TM

Project Director:	Dana F. Kellerman
Editors:	Catherine M. Lang Elizabeth J. Ryan
Copy Editor:	Estella M. Kawaky
Staff Assistants:	Patricia A. Johnson Janet C. Katien Jo T. Novak
Consultant:	Lloyd A. Besant
Designers:	Suzanne Sumner James E. Kelly, Jr.

The editors are grateful to Elaine Katz and Charles H. Montague for providing some of the practice material used in the student workbook.

SRA edition

TM

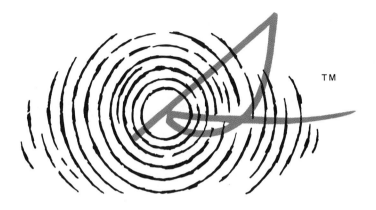

STENOSCRIPT®

abc

shorthand

ISBN: 0–574–15001–3

17

SRA® SCIENCE RESEARCH ASSOCIATES, INC.
Chicago, Henley-on-Thames, Sydney, Toronto

A Subsidiary of IBM

Introduction

The shorthand system you are about to learn is Stenoscript® ABC Shorthand. It is a system based on the letters of the alphabet and common punctuation symbols. Because it is easy to learn and easy to write, you can begin writing Stenoscript on the first day of your class instruction. You will be able to master the entire theory of Stenoscript in a fraction of the time you would require to learn systems of shorthand based on nonalphabetic symbols. By regular, sustained practice you will attain the speed needed for office dictation and for a variety of other notetaking situations. Many Stenoscript students have reached a speed of 120 words a minute. Furthermore, because there are no unusual or special symbols, your shorthand will be legible and easy to transcribe, by you or by anyone else who knows the system, even months after you have written it. In addition, if need or convenience requires it, your Stenoscript notes can be taken on the typewriter.

The forty rules of the Stenoscript system can be summarized briefly as follows:

1. The symbols of Stenoscript® ABC Shorthand are the letters of the alphabet, the slant mark, the dash, and the comma.

2. When you hear the name of a letter of the alphabet at the beginning or end of a word, write that letter. For example, in the sound of the word *easy* you hear the two letters e and z, so you write ez.

3. Vowels drop out, except at the beginning and end of words, and as noted below.

4. Most long vowels followed by a final single consonant sound are retained. You will learn to recognize this long-vowel sound quickly.

5. The letters *l* and *r* often drop out.

6. There are short forms to memorize for words and sounds of high frequency in the English language.

The Stenoscript ABC Shorthand Business Word List at the back of this book contains all the words used in the exercises. The majority of the more than 6000 entries are among the most common words used in business and industry.

This manual presents the forty rules of Stenoscript—individually, with examples and practice words. The Practice sections in each chapter list words that you are to write in Stenoscript, applying in particular the rule that the list accompanies. After you have checked your exercises for accuracy, be sure to rewrite several times the forms you wrote incorrectly. If you missed a form that was presented under an earlier rule, go back and review the rule and the practice words that accompany it.

It is extremely important that you commit to memory the High-Frequency Word List presented in the first four chapters. The words listed are among those that occur most often in our speaking and writing. You will encounter them repeatedly in this text and in the dictation exercises your teacher will give you.

The Review section in each chapter is devoted to reinforcement and recall. It is designed to improve your grasp of the principles covered in the chapter and to strengthen skills developed in earlier chapters. It is also diagnostic in nature: the words you miss in any part of the Review section will tell you what rules you should review and whether you need to spend more time on the High-Frequency Word List. Part I is a word drill for the rules treated in the chapter and in preceding chapters. Part II and Part III provide practice in writing connected material (sentences and paragraphs or letters). Part IV, the transcription exercise, gives you practice in reading Stenoscript. You will discover that the meaning of a form, no matter how perplexing it may seem standing alone, becomes readily apparent in the context of a connected sentence or paragraph.

Stenoscript shorthand can be written on a lined tablet, in a looseleaf notebook, or on a memo pad, or it can be typed on typing paper. For this course, however, you will be required to use a standard shorthand notebook and a ballpoint pen. Choose a pen that writes smoothly and is well adapted to your handwriting. Always have a spare pen at hand. Write on every line of the notebook, to the dividing line that runs down the center of the page. This will give you two columns of writing to a page. Write on one side of the page only. If you make a mistake, do not erase. Strike out the error with a single stroke of your pen, and write the correct form. When you have written on all the pages, turn the notebook over and write on the reverse of each page, from the back to the front of the book. In order not to lose time turning pages, slide each page upward as you write the second column so that when you finish the page you can flip it over with a quick motion and be ready to write on the top line of the next page. Do this even when you are not doing speed exercises, so that you will establish good habits from the first day of your course. Be sure to keep your writing area free of clutter.

Since Stenoscript is based on the way a word sounds, it is important that you **hear** the words and exercises you are writing. When you are working from your book, **say** the words as you write them, aloud if circumstances permit, otherwise by moving your lips and pronouncing them mentally.

When you first begin to write in Stenoscript, you will be thinking about the sounds you are hearing and the forms you are writing. You will be making a **conscious** association between sound and symbol. Later, as you practice and build skill, the sound-to-symbol process will no longer be conscious. It will be **automatic.** It is at this point, when your Stenoscript becomes automatic, that you will be moving into the speeds that will make Stenoscript a really useful tool for you.

Constant and sustained practice is therefore extremely important. Your teacher will give you timed dictation drills in class. Be sure to follow her recommendations and suggestions on how to build up your dictation speeds outside class.

Contents

Chapter 1

You are about to begin the first chapter of STENOSCRIPT® ABC SHORTHAND. As you make progress in the book, you will be learning a set of rules that, with practice, should enable you to gain a writing speed of 100 or even 120 words a minute. Stenoscript is an easy system to master, but to gain speed you must practice regularly.

1. Write vowel sounds at the beginning or end of a word. Do not write vowel sounds within a word. (Exceptions will be noted in later chapters.)

animal	*anml*	cider	*sdr*	ledger	*lyr*
array	*ara*	cipher	*sfr*	level	*lvl*
borrow	*bro*	differ	*dfr*	open	*opn*
cab	*kb*	item	*ilm*	pie	*pi*
cage	*kj*	job	*jb*	ticket	*tkt*
censor	*snsr*	lay	*la*	unit	*unt*

Write the following:

j when you hear the j sound as in *job* and *ledger*
f when you hear the f̄ sound as in *cipher*
k when you hear the k̲ sound as in *cab*
s when you hear the s̲ sound as in *cider*

Notice in the examples above that in Stenoscript the *t* is not crossed, and the *i* and *j* are not dotted. The reason is that in order to gain speed in taking dictation, your hand should always move in a forward direction. To distinguish between *t* and *l* and between *i* and e, be sure to close letters *t* and *i* and loop letters *l* and e. Write these letters as follows:

t ___; l ___; i ___; e ___; j ___.

Be sure to loop the *j* and close the small *s* so they cannot be confused with the comma, which is also a symbol used in Stenoscript.

2

Practice

above	damage	maze
amaze	eager	metal
auto	egg	newspaper
back	error	notice
because	favor	package
bitten	fellow	recess
book	few	review
bottom	give	rose
cancel	good	sell
cater	judge	size
cigar	matter	some

Did you notice that certain words, such as *book* and *back,* are written the same way in Stenoscript? In transcribing actual dictation, you will be able to determine the correct word from the context of the sentence in which it is used. For example:

Put the *bk* on the table.
Put it *bk* on the table.

2. When the initial or final sound of a word is the name of a letter of the alphabet, write that letter. (Remember: do not write vowel sounds within a word.)

argue	rgu	else	ls	icy	ic
easy	ez	enemy	nme	sunny	sne

Practice

candy	funny	ivy
city	happy	money
encourage	heavy	regency
fancy	honey	wise

3. When a base word ends in a double consonant sound, write the first of the two sounds. (Later rules will either build on or modify this rule.)

adopt	adp	expect	xpk	task	ts
direct	drk	loft	lf	text	tx

Practice

desk	except	next
detect	fact	object
eject	left	soft

4. Whenever *d* or *ed* is added to a base word, underline the last letter or symbol.

adopt	adp	adopted	adp
borrow	bro	borrowed	bro
detect	dtk	detected	dtk
fix	fx	fixed	fx

Practice

accepted	caused	directed
amazed	damaged	objected
catered	defied	reviewed

5. In Stenoscript a plural word ending in *s* or *es* is written the same as the singular form. The context of the sentence should indicate whether the word is singular or plural.

animal anml animals anml

cab kb cabs kb

cigar sgr cigars sgr

package pkj packages pkj

(If after you have learned and practiced the 40 rules of Stenoscript you are still having trouble identifying plural words, you may find it helpful to place a small dot under the final letter of the Stenoscript form to identify it as a plural form. For example, *cars* could be written kr, and *women* could be written wmn.)

Verbs that form their third-person singular by adding *s* or *es* also drop this final sound in Stenoscript.

borrow bro borrows bro

pay pa pays pa

run rn runs rn

sell sl sells sl

Note, however, that three frequently used third-person singular words—*has, says,* and *does*—are written *hz, sz,* and *dz.*

6. Use regular punctuation. Do not use the hyphen.

To indicate a new paragraph, use two long slant marks (//) and then continue writing on the same line.

7. You may use any common abbreviation that is shorter than the Stenoscript form. For example, since the standard abbreviation for *manager* *(mgr)* is shorter than the Stenoscript form *(mnjr),* you may prefer to use the standard abbreviation.

   Write figures for numbers except *one,* which is written *wn.* However, very large rounded numbers, such as *million* and *billion,* are treated as words. For example, *three billion* would be written *3 bln.*

8. There are approximately 120 words that occur with great frequency in written and spoken language. These words are called high-frequency words and are an important part of any shorthand system. Mastery of the list of high-frequency words will greatly increase the speed with which you can write Stenoscript. The list has been divided into four groups to facilitate memorization and practice. One group appears in each of the first four chapters of this manual.

High-Frequency Word List—Group I

a an	*a*
and	*+*
be been being by bye buy but	*b*
see seen seeing	*c*
do due did done doing	*d*
day	*D*
he me	*e*
for	*f*
go goes gone going	*g*
had have having	*h*
I	*I*
if it its is	*i*
can come came coming	*k*

REVIEW

I. Words. Write the Stenoscript for the following.

1. adopt
2. coming
3. get
4. having
5. review
6. package
7. some
8. next
9. me
10. autos
11. cipher
12. he
13. level
14. judge
15. but
16. manager
17. due
18. damaged
19. animal
20. have
21. eject
22. be
23. pie
24. see
25. differ
26. buy
27. fact
28. eyes
29. came
30. did
31. maze
32. caged
33. eggs
34. it
35. and
36. gone
37. for
38. has
39. fixed
40. if
41. censor
42. goes
43. regency
44. done
45. object
46. catered
47. been
48. a
49. amazed
50. back
51. city
52. seeing
53. day
54. roses

II. Sentences. Write the Stenoscript for the following.

1. I have a book. It is a good book, but I have had a better book.
2. It is an easy task and I can do it.
3. He is having it fixed.
4. Did he get a package?
5. He came for me, but I had gone.
6. See if he has some roses I can buy.
7. He left me a ticket, but I have some.
8. I have seen a funny metal object.
9. I recall seeing some tickets and a package.
10. If I see a good book, I can buy it.

III. Paragraphs. Write the Stenoscript for the following.

1. I can use a pencil. He can buy me a pencil. I can use a pen. If he goes, see if he can get me a pen. See if he can buy me some paper when he gets me a pen. If he gets me a pencil, a pen, and some paper, I can pay for it.

2. He has a dog. It is a big dog. If it is a good dog, he can buy it some liver. If it is a bad dog, he can sell it. If I see a good dog, I pet it. If I see a bad dog, I run.

IV. Transcription. Transcribe the following.

I h a kr. i i a gd kr wn i
rn. i hz a gd mtr. i i g bd,
I k h i fx. i e b i, e k pa e
f i. i I c a btr kr, I k b i.
I h sm mne + I k pa f i.

Chapter 2

9. Write the small letter c when you hear the ch sound.

attach alc catch kc chop cp

teacher lcr

Practice

choose	kitchen	such
coach	much	teach
detach	reach	watch

10. Use a dash (——) to represent the word *the* and the sounds of *th, nd, nt, mand, mend,* and *ment*. Connect the dash to the letter preceding or following it in the word.

a) The sound of *th*

bath b— other o—r then —n

Practice

beneath	father	than
both	feather	that
death	gather	their
either	leather	them

b) The sounds of *nd, nt, mand, mend,* and *ment*

kind k—　　demand d—　　cement s—

sent s—　　amend a—

Practice

account	expand	resident
attend	extend	round
event	gentle	sound
evident	patent	want

If a word requires two adjoining dashes, connect the two dashes with a slight jog:

amendment a——

Practice

attendant	dependent	pendant
defendant	descendant	redundant

Use the Stenoscript of the base word. You have learned to drop the vowels within words when writing Stenoscript. However, when a word is **built on** another word that ends in a vowel sound, keep this vowel sound of the base word when you write the Stenoscript. For example:

Base word	Word built on the base word
rely rli	reliant rli—
pay pa	payment pa—

How would you write *defiant* in Stenoscript?

11. Write the small letter *g* when you hear the ng sound.

among amg angle agl eating elg

Practice

along	hanging	saying
backing	hung	selling
boxing	judging	single
chopping	longing	something
demanding	paying	wrong

Did you remember to write the vowel in the Stenoscript for *paying*? for *saying*? Remember, they were words **built on** base words.

10 12. Write the small letter *j* when you hear the shun, chun, or zhun sound.

action akj attention alnj question qsj

fashion fj occasion okj relation rlj

Practice

definition	nation	selection
edition	notation	session
location	ocean	suggestion
mention	position	vision
motion	section	vocation

13. Write the small letter *z* when you hear the sh or zh sound.

fish fz measure mzr ship zp

issue izu patient pz

Practice

ancient	lash	shell
cash	leash	shoe
deficient	leisure	shop
diminish	push	show
dish	rush	wish

14. Use the small letter *q* to represent the nk sound and the qu letter-group sound.

    a) The nk sound

    bank *bq* link *lq*

Practice

function	sink	think
rank	thank	wrinkle

b) The qu letter-group sound

equal *eql* quit *ql*

Practice

acquit	qualify	quiz
liquid	quiver	sequel

15. Do not write an *l* if the l sound occurs **within** a base word and is preceded or followed by a different consonant sound.

    clever *kvr* told *ld*

Practice

black	flush	plan
blow	glass	play
clinic	gold	sold

Write the *l* within a word if *l* is doubled (*ll*) or if it occurs between two vowels.

follow flo value vlu

Practice

belong	develop	pillow
cellar	dollar	pilot
color	elect	regular
delay	fellow	sell
deliver	hollow	solid

16. Do not write an *r* if the r sound occurs **within** a base word and is preceded or followed by a different consonant sound.

farmer fmr pretend pl

Practice

bring	forget	purchase
brother	former	purse
critic	product	service
cross	promise	traffic
forbid	protect	truck

Write the *r* within a word if *r* is doubled (*rr*) or if it occurs between two vowels.

barrel brl carol krl

Practice

caress	current	parent
carriage	enrich	quarrel
carrot	hero	rural
chorus	merit	series
courage	oral	sorrow

all
well
will — *l*

mine
my
am
him
many — *m*

month — *M*

in
neither
know
no
none
nor
not — *n*

or
on
owe
so — *o*

out — *O*

up — *p*

are
her
hers
our
ours
hour — *r*

saw
us — *s*

at
to
too — *t*

the — —

I. Words. Write the Stenoscript for the following.

1. eager
2. else
3. sounded
4. will
5. recess
6. happy
7. gentle
8. well
9. judge
10. agency
11. payments
12. all
13. some
14. detect
15. finding
16. none
17. have
18. desk
19. something
20. not
21. can
22. runs
23. section
24. nor
25. be
26. catch
27. education
28. neither
29. goes
30. much
31. possession
32. know
33. come
34. the
35. fishing
36. no
37. if
38. death
39. quiet
40. in
41. issue
42. back
43. favor
44. him
45. notice
46. sell
47. forget
48. many
49. cross
50. alarmed
51. shoe
52. am
53. leather
54. blank
55. watched
56. my
57. play
58. accounts
59. service
60. crew
61. quick
62. glass
63. blue
64. helps
65. product
66. thank
67. at
68. us
69. them
70. bent
71. argue
72. caress

II. Sentences. Write the Stenoscript for the following.

1. He can reach the chopped wood.
2. If he is talking, I can pay the check.
3. The older hotel has excellent service.
4. I showed her my matchbook cover collection.
5. The metal box is bigger and better than the wooden box.
6. The teacher told me to go to the office for the book.
7. This lesson is easy, but you have to pay attention.
8. I think that I am going to the carnival.
9. Show me a quick way to get this done.
10. The payment came this morning.

III. Paragraphs. Write the Stenoscript for the following.

1. He told me to buy all the books. He said that he would pay me. I know that he pays the bills for the book account.

2. The coach chooses the men and teaches them to play ball. They learn to catch and to throw and to run well. They do not miss practice because they want to learn to play better. The coach tells them that if they practice well, they will win.

3. I think the office is being managed well. The man that runs the office for me is an excellent manager. The new man will learn the job if he observes the manager. I will go with him if I can. It would be a good way for me to see if things are going well.

4. The man has a new teaching position. He teaches in the building they opened in the fall. He does the job well because he is a good teacher. He is not harsh, but he is firm and the class respects him. For this reason, he is respected by the mothers and fathers too. The pupils he teaches will get a good education. The other parents wish their children could be in that class.

IV. Transcription. Transcribe the following.

ppl fm m nj k l r l — l lv.
—a k f m dfr— rzn, b —a h
wn rzn n kmn. —a k bkz
—a r lkg f a btr wa l lv.
i i n lwz ez bkz —a h mc l
ln, b wn —a bk slzn —a r
hp.

Chapter 3

17. Use a slant mark (/) to represent the sounds of *rd, rt,* and *rk* and the letter group *ward*.

a) The sound of *rd*

accord  harder  order 

guard 

Notice that when the slant is used within a word, as in *harder* and *order*, you continue writing at the top of the slant.

Practice

afford	cards	record
bird	garden	regard
board	hard	yard
burden	pardon	word

b) The sound of *rt*

alert *al/* effort *f/* exported *xp/*

apartment *ap/*

Notice the way the slant is underlined in the Stenoscript for the word *exported* to show the *ed* ending.

Practice

assert	expert	reported
court	hurt	reverted
department	mortal	sorted
deport	quarter	supported

c) The sound of *rk*

dark *d/* marking *m/g*

Practice

clerk	remarking	turkey
network	spark	work
park	sparkle	working

d) The *ward* letter group

backward *bk/* outward *o/* warden */n*

Practice

awarding	inward	upward
forward	rewarding	wayward

18. Use the small letter *y* to represent the *ry* and *rry* letter groups (pronounced ree) at the end of words, and the oi sound.

a) The *ry* and *rry* letter groups

battery bly directory drky sorry sy

century sncy

Practice

carry	hurry	salary
dairy	jury	summary
delivery	luxury	supervisory
grocery	misery	worry

b) The oi sound

annoy any employed mpy point py

choice cys

Practice

appoint	foil	loyal
boy	invoice	royal
coin	joined	soil
enjoyed	joint	voice

19. Write the small letter *m* when you hear the sound of *mis* or *im* at the beginning of a word.

a) The sound of *mis*

misfit mfl misspend msp misuse muz

Notice that when *mis* is added to a word that begins with a vowel sound, as in *misuse,* you must write the vowel of the base word.

Practice

misapply	misdirect	misjudge
misbehave	misgiving	mislay
misbrand	mishandle	mismatch
miscount	mishap	misspell

b) The sound of *im*

image *mj* impress *mps*

Practice

imagination	impel	imprint
imagine	imperfect	improper
imitation	impressed	improve
impact	impressive	improvement

However, for words that begin with the letters *imm,* write *im*. For example, the word *immortal* is written *im/l*. Now write the Stenoscript for these words.

immaterial	immigrant	immoderate
immerse	immigration	immoral

20. Write the small letter *d* when you hear the dis or des sound at the beginning of a word.

description *dkpj* disagree *dage* discuss *dks*

desperate *dprl*

Practice

desperation	disappoint	disengage
despise	discard	disfavor
despondent	discount	dismiss
despotic	discover	disorder

Did you remember to write the a in *disappoint* and the o in *disorder?*

21. Use the following special abbreviations for the salutation and the complimentary close of a letter.

a) The salutation

Dear d	Gentlemen g	Dear Miss dmi
Dear Sir ds	Dear Mr. dmr	Dear Mrs. dms
Dear Madam dm		

b) The complimentary close

Cordially c	Sincerely s	Yours truly ul
Cordially yours cu	Sincerely yours su	Yours very truly uvl
Respectfully r	Yours sincerely us	Very truly yours vlu

These abbreviations are used **only** for the salutation and close of a letter. The word *sir,* for example, is written *sr* except when it is part of the phrase *Dear Sir.*

High-Frequency Word List—Group III

you your yours	u	over	V	why	y
under	U	we were who whom	w	year	Y
of very	v	week	W	as was his she	z

REVIEW

I. Words. Write the Stenoscript for the following.

1. guard
2. our
3. voice
4. she
5. discount
6. century
7. under
8. expert
9. misdirect
10. over
11. why
12. he
13. by
14. on
15. her
16. watch
17. gentle
18. ocean
19. function
20. cellar
21. protect
22. mishandling
23. parking
24. inward
25. your
26. hurry
27. who
28. department
29. at
30. am
31. sparkle
32. imprint
33. very
34. his
35. were
36. in
37. feather
38. single
39. pushing
40. wrinkle
41. critic
42. carriage
43. up
44. reporting
45. shorthand
46. of
47. loyal
48. so
49. whom
50. upward
51. as
52. discovery
53. or
54. him
55. impel
56. was
57. saw
58. cement
59. paying
60. position
61. qualify
62. played
63. carry

II. Sentences. Write the Stenoscript for the following.

1. We want to thank you for your recent order.
2. It was hard work and there was no easy way to do it.
3. There were some other papers that I wanted to send with the letter.
4. I am going to work for the Pardon Board.
5. The personnel department has a report on the guard.
6. Will you please send us your check for the bill?
7. The regular program on education drew the issue to our attention.
8. The truck traveled in heavy traffic to deliver the cement to the shop.
9. This is a message to tell you that we are pleased with the large order you sent us.
10. If we do not have a reply from you, we will ship the goods tomorrow.

III. Paragraphs. Write the Stenoscript for the following.

1.
Dear Sir:

We wish to discuss your bill with you. If you will come to our office, we can finish all the work and send the report to the billing department without delay. Thank you.

Sincerely,

2.
Gentlemen:

We have notified you of our choice for the position of general manager and we have had no further word from you.

We want to know if you support us in this matter, as your approval is very important for this appointment.

Yours very truly,

3.
Dear Madam:

We are happy to say that our market will deliver groceries. You can call and your groceries will be delivered to you. You should not worry that your order will be mishandled. Our delivery boy is an expert in handling groceries.

We are certain that you will enjoy using this service.

Very truly yours,

4.
Dear Bob,

Thank you for your invitation to attend the opening of your play. I know we will enjoy it. It is kind of you to ask us. We will see you there.

Sincerely,

5.
Dear Sir:

You will want to have your car in good running order for all kinds of weather. Why not let our experts look it over for you? It can be picked up at your office and returned to you. There is no charge for this service. You will be billed for the materials used and there will be a small fee for labor. Come in and see us.

Yours truly,

IV. Transcription. Transcribe the following.

ds: — q u f u rs — or. i k n — s
mng + w l s — i O wg dla. w
l lu l gl — o — r — g u w — s l ck
o f u. w l n s — — m l u wg
llg u n. pz lls n — nmbr v — z
ilm u l w — . i u w — z m z 100,
w k d mc blr f u. vlu,

Chapter 4

24

22. The long-vowel rule. When the final single consonant sound of a base word is preceded by a long-vowel sound, **write the vowel sound** when you write the word, but **drop** the final consonant sound.

The long-vowel sounds are the a, e, i, o, and u sounds as they are heard in the following words. Say them as you read them.

a as in *brake* ba

e as in *cheap* ce

i as in *fine* fi

o as in *home* ho

u as in *soon* su or *mute* mu

Practice

Say these words to yourself as you write them so that you will get used to recognizing the long-vowel sounds when you hear them.

alone
aloof
belief
clean
deduce
deed
expire
face
fake
fame
file
fire
hope
knife
late
leaf
life
like
loaf
loose
made
moon
neat
niece
night
plane
pole
price
rate
ream
receipt
remain
ride
rope
routine
rude
rule
safe
sale
scheme
shade
shame
shape
shoot
side
smile
suit
take
tape
time
train
tune
type
vote

Here are some examples of long vowels in longer words. Remember that they come just before the final consonant sound.

educate *ejka* expedite *xpdi* nominate *nmna*

Practice

appetite
calculate
celebrate
dominate
eliminate
irritate
midnight
parasite
penetrate

There is an exception to the long-vowel rule. When the final consonant is a j sound, v sound, or z sound, write these sounds instead of the long-vowel sound.

For example:

cage *kj* leave *lv* rose *rz*

Practice

achieve	freeze	rave
behave	fuse	receive
believe	move	save
blaze	praise	tease
cave	rage	wage
chose	raise	weave

26

Now try these words. Remember to **write** the long vowel **unless** it is followed by a j sound, v sound, or z sound. Say the words as you write them.

brave	gauge	relieve
breeze	hike	remove
broke	lane	retain
chief	load	robe
erase	mail	role
exclude	nice	smoke
expose	piece	trade
feel	race	vote
froze	reduce	waive

23. **Write the vowel sound** but **drop** the *r* when you write words that end in the following letter-group sounds: ar as in *fair,* er as in *here,* or as in *roar,* and ur as in *poor.*

For example:

the ar sound when you pronounce	-air	as in	*fair*	fa
	-are	as in	*care*	ka
	-ear	as in	*wear*	wa
the er sound when you pronounce	-ere	as in	*here*	he
	-eer	as in	*cheer*	ce
	-ier	as in	*pier*	pe
	-ear	as in	*near*	ne
the or sound when you pronounce	-oar	as in	*roar*	ro
	-ore	as in	*more*	mo
	-oor	as in	*door*	do
	-our	as in	*pour*	po
the ur sound when you pronounce	-ure	as in	*sure*	zu
	-our	as in	*tour*	lu
	-oor	as in	*poor*	pu

Practice

affair	bare	boar
appear	bear	brochure

career	engineer	score
chair	fare	severe
chore	fear	share
clear	floor	sheer
core	insure	sincere
cure	mature	soar
dare	moor	sore
dear	pear	tier
declare	peer	tore
detour	rare	ware
endure	repair	wear

Exceptions to this rule are the following short words:

air ___ar___ oar ___or___ ore ___or___

ear ___er___

24. Write the capital letter *S* when you hear the <u>st</u> letter-group sound.

estate ___eSa___ sister ___sSr___ test ___tS___

stop ___Sp___

Practice

arrest	fast	register
assist	historical	rest
best	instrument	restrict
blast	invest	rust
capitalist	just	staff
cast	journalist	stand
cost	lost	stem
crust	mast	still
destination	mistrust	stock
destruction	most	twist
domestic	novelist	vast
enlist	persist	wrist
establish	protest	youngster

Word	Outline
about	
after	af
again, against	ag
any	ne
began, begin, beginning, begun	bg
even, ever, every	ev
from	fm
off, often	of
one	wn
never	nv
that	—t
their, there	—r
these	—z
they	—a
this	—s
those	—oz
upon	pn
where	wa
which	wc
whose	wz
with	w—
without	

I. Words. Write the Stenoscript for the following.

1. appoint
2. every
3. detachment
4. begin
5. location
6. those
7. diminish
8. upon
9. wrinkled
10. began
11. regular
12. any
13. process
14. there
15. current
16. repair
17. protection
18. again
19. store
20. never
21. still
22. this
23. steer
24. beginning
25. enlistment
26. roar
27. price
28. they
29. remain
30. after
31. educate
32. was
33. save
34. you
35. mail
36. carry
37. their
38. sacrifice
39. often
40. receive
41. that
42. engage
43. least
44. feel
45. fell
46. leave
47. very
48. against
49. without
50. nice
51. these
52. undermine
53. extreme
54. hurry
55. remove
56. vote
57. word
58. off
59. exclude
60. with
61. care
62. ever
63. more
64. work
65. order
66. which
67. near
68. from
69. where
70. mistake
71. chore
72. test
73. whose
74. oblige
75. even
76. estate
77. estimate
78. begun
79. include
80. destroy
81. forgave

II. Sentences. Write the Stenoscript for the following.

1. His fame as a dedicated public servant is widespread.
2. His secretary ordered the roses for the reception.
3. The repairman was ready to stop work when the bell rang for lunch.
4. The assistant to the department head calculated the amount of the bill so that the package could be expedited.
5. The gas tank registered empty and we still had miles to go before arriving at our destination.

6. It is a shame that there will not be any officers of that group at the formal meeting.
7. The secretary of state spoke before a meeting of citizens to describe national policy on the war issue.
8. He will make any sacrifice to achieve his goal of fiscal reform.
9. The president of the firm declared that discrimination in hiring had been eliminated.
10. He misjudges his manager when he thinks the work of the parts repair section is being mishandled.

III. Paragraphs. Write the Stenoscript for the following.

1.
Gentlemen:

I would like to express my high regard for your excellent cheese product. It is the best cheese I have ever purchased. The taste is different and pleasing. I have just ordered several dozen packages to be sent to friends as Christmas gifts.

I thought you would be pleased to hear from a happy customer.

Sincerely yours,

2.
Dear Sir:

Your request for a description of an electric stapling machine arrived in the morning mail. We would like very much to help you, but do not carry this machine. We would suggest that you discuss this matter with some large office equipment firm. They will be well prepared to give you the description you need, and perhaps to arrange for a demonstration.

Yours very truly,

3.
Dear Mary,

I am writing to ask you to help me plan a trip. Dick and I want to go to Mexico this fall, and we have many questions. You are the expert on Mexico, so we thought you might have some suggestions. Should we go by train or by air? Train travel is more relaxed. We would have time to enjoy the landscape and make friends. On the other hand, making the trip by air would be much faster and would give us more time in Mexico. What do you think?

After we arrive in Mexico, we expect to rent a car. Perhaps you would help us with suggestions of places to visit. Do you have the names of some good hotels? With lots of atmosphere, of course!

Last but not least, Mary, we need to keep the cost of this trip to a minimum. Any hints for saving money will be most welcome.

Many thanks for your help. Regards to Tom and the children.

Sincerely,

4.
Dear Sir:

Our accounting office has just forwarded to us a statement showing that your account is past due. According to our records, you have not made the last two payments on your loan.

Our credit policy is liberal, and we think the terms of our agreement with you are fair. However, if you lack cash to make your payments as stipulated, we are willing to discuss new terms. Perhaps an extension of your loan would be in order.

Please stop in or write and let us know the terms under which you could begin to repay the amount you owe. You will find that our credit officers are understanding and ready to help in whatever way they can. May we expect to hear from you soon?

Very truly yours,

5.
Dear Mrs. Jones:

We are sorry to notify you that the dishes you ordered are out of stock. May we suggest another nice pattern? It is called Even Glow, and it has been very popular with many of our discriminating customers. You will find pictures of this pattern and a description of all the pieces in the enclosed illustrated catalog. It comes in blue, pink, and lavender. The list price is the same as the price of the pattern you ordered. Now, however, during our June sale, we can offer you a 10-percent discount.

We are sure you will not be disappointed with Even Glow. We will be pleased to process your order as soon as it reaches our office. May we hear from you by return mail?

Yours very truly,

IV. Transcription. Transcribe the following.

i u li a rfzg dg, u l w— l li
nu b— sf dg. nu b— i a nu kbna
dg ma fm— fiS dSl wlr, n —
keS, mS mdn bllg p— n — wd.
u l lS re fu for n nu b—. nu
bu lS blr bkz i i blr. b nu b— —
nx li u g zpg. u hzb— + u cdn
l — g u + u f l — g u r a
pfk hSs.

Chapter 5

25. Memorize the 24 brief forms listed below. These brief forms do not necessarily conform to the rules of Stenoscript.

accompany	ac	company	co	opportunity	op
accomplish	ac	corporate	crp	organize	og
acknowledge	ak	government	gvt	particular	prt
administer	adm	immediate	imd	represent	rp
appreciate	ap	individual	ndv	responsible	rsp
approximate	apx	information	nfo	satisfy	st
associate	as	manufacture	mf	situation	sit
business	bz	merchandise	mds	specify	spc

Use each brief form for all forms of the word it represents. For example, the various forms of *acknowledge* would all be written as follows:

acknowledge
acknowledged
acknowledging
acknowledgment } *ak*

All the forms of *organize* would be written *og* . The context of the sentence will tell you which form is meant.

organize
organized
organizer
organization
organizational
organizing
organizable } *og*

Now try writing the brief form for each of the following words.

association	representative	representing
corporation	administration	satisfactory
immediate	accompanied	immediately
manufacturer	corporative	merchandising
situation	individual	satisfaction
governmental	particularly	responsibility
accomplish	responsible	specification
company	approximate	accomplishing
individually	organization	informational
opportunity	information	representation
administrative	merchandise	specify
approximately	appreciation	associate
particular	manufactured	specific

All the high-frequency words that you memorized in the first four chapters are listed on this and the facing page for reference and review.

a
an

and

be
been
being
by
bye
buy
but

see
seen
seeing

do
due
did
done
doing

day

he
me

for

go
goes
gone
going

had
have
having

I

if
it
its
is

can
come
came
coming

all
well
will

mine
my
am
him
many

month

in
neither
know
no
none
nor
not

or
on
owe
so

out

up

are
her
hers
our
ours
hour

saw
us

at
to
too

the	—
you your yours	u
under	U
of very	v
over	V
we were who whom	w
week	W
why	y
year	Y
as was his she	z
about	ao
after	af
again against	ag
any	ne
began begin beginning begun	bg
even ever every	ev
from	fm
off often	of
one	wn
never	nv
that	—t
their there	—r
these	—z
they	—a
this	—s
those	—oz
upon	pn
where	wa
which	wc
whose	wz
with	w—
without	w—o

REVIEW

I. Words. Write the Stenoscript for the following.

1. situation
2. done
3. for
4. a
5. the
6. in
7. go
8. mine
9. an
10. year
11. too
12. no
13. gone
14. him
15. and
16. he
17. know
18. to
19. going
20. many
21. be
22. accomplish
23. you
24. she
25. after
26. never
27. upon
28. which
29. whose
30. his
31. week
32. again
33. any
34. by
35. see
36. am
37. my
38. owe
39. not
40. as
41. we
42. they
43. begin
44. with
45. month
46. had
47. nor
48. saw
49. her
50. up
51. at
52. under
53. of
54. against
55. this
56. that
57. over
58. who
59. why
60. was
61. those
62. did
63. it
64. day
65. so
66. neither
67. goes
68. being
69. began
70. ever
71. often
72. these
73. very
74. yours
75. begun
76. been
77. having
78. if
79. will
80. are
81. or
82. none
83. all
84. can
85. have
86. seen
87. due
88. off
89. there
90. appreciate
91. from
92. were
93. business
94. buy
95. every
96. individual
97. even
98. whom
99. opportunity
100. out
101. about
102. do
103. represent
104. on
105. come
106. satisfy
107. corporation
108. immediately

II. Sentences. Write the Stenoscript for the following.

1. The national organization will handle all hotel reservations, but each individual is responsible for making his own travel arrangements.
2. If you are not satisfied with the merchandise, the company will refund your money.
3. An individual should be appointed who would be responsible for administering the self-education program.
4. These meetings provide an excellent opportunity for managers of small businesses to exchange information about similar problems.
5. There are approximately ten manufacturers who could make this product according to our specifications.
6. Every questionnaire should be accompanied by a form letter explaining the purpose of this study.
7. We must find a solution to the present situation immediately.
8. Each company has been asked to send at least one representative to the meeting on business-government relations.
9. We were particularly pleased to learn that you do appreciate the difficulty of the situation.
10. Who is responsible for obtaining detailed information about the corporate structure of the company?

III. Paragraphs. Write the Stenoscript for the following.

1.
Dear Mr. Ray:

We welcome this opportunity to assist the government in planning the nationwide study of vocational rehabilitation. While the task is an enormous one, we feel that with good organization it can be accomplished within the time allotted and with a minimum amount of difficulty. We would therefore like to meet with representatives from your department this week so that we may begin planning immediately.

Sincerely,

2.
Some pairs of words that express opposing meanings are the following: over and under, in and out, before and after, for and against, this and that, these and those, many and few, every and none, particular and general, begin and end, go and come, buy and sell, acknowledge and ignore, either and neither, or and nor, ever and never, business and pleasure.

On the other hand, some pairs of words that express similar meanings are the following: accomplish and do, manufacture and make, pleased and satisfied, immediate and present, approximate and near, appreciate and thank, personal and individual, merchandise and goods, association and company.

3.
The American Tool and Die Corporation has just released to the press the information that it plans to organize a branch in Richmond, Virginia. Robert Smith, who has been associated with American Tool and Die for the entire period between its incorporation in 1947 and the present, has been named vice-president and will be responsible for organizing and administering the new branch.

American Tool and Die manufactures small machine parts for printing presses. Its principal customers are the federal government and large manufacturing companies in the Atlantic states.

Smith, 49, lives in Washington with his wife and four children. He plans to move to Richmond in June.

4.
Dear Mr. Johnson:

The accompanying brochure will give you the information that you requested about the development seminar for personnel administration managers. As you will see, the seminar has been organized in two parts to satisfy the particular needs of individuals in many situations.

The first part covers the policy responsibilities of the personnel officer, gives information that will help him understand what policy is, the way it is made and administered, and what the key personnel issues are today.

The second part of the seminar discusses the role of the personnel officer and his relationship with management. It deals with such topics as the nature of staff positions, how to determine the standards for staff personnel officers, and how to improve individual accomplishments in staff positions through better delegation, organization, and management of time.

If you wish to participate in this seminar, we suggest that you apply immediately, because registration is limited to fifteen individuals.

Very truly yours,

IV. Transcription. Transcribe the following.

dmr jnz: z u rqs, bb sm—, r
co rp n u dSk, l b klg o u o Ma
12 l dks u mds pbm. // mr. sm—
hz b as w— r mf co f m Y &
i fmlr w— — opry v sml bz. e
l sp— — afnu w—u, dksg —
pbm v u prl bz n — ho v kag
a mo sl sa sil f u. vlu,

Chapter 6

26. Write the small letter *k* when you hear the sound of *com, con,* or *counter* at the beginning of a word.

commerce kms confirm kfm contract klk

compact kpk connect knk counteract kak

Practice

combat	concern	contradict
commission	condemn	control
compass	connection	counterattack
compel	consent	counterfeit
compete	constant	counterpart

27. Write the capital letter *N* when you hear the sound of *enter, entr, inter,* or *intr* at the beginning of a word.

enter N interpret Npl introduction Ndkj

entry Ne

Practice

entering	interject	interval
enterprise	intermediate	interview
intercept	intermix	interworking
interim	international	introductory

28. Write the capital letter *B* when you hear the ble sound at the end of a word.

able *aB* libel *lB* possible *psB*

symbol *smB*

Practice

Bible	enable	legible
cable	feeble	rebel
capable	impossible	stable
disable	incapable	table
double	label	trouble

In some words ending with the ble sound, the sound of the base word is heard. In such cases, write the Stenoscript for the base word and then add the capital *B*. For example:

agree *age* agreeable *ageB*

desire *dzi* desirable *dziB*

vary *vy* variable *vyB*

Now try to write the Stenoscript for these words.

deniable	justifiable	reliable
disagreeable	notable	suitable
identifiable	peaceable	verifiable

29. Use a comma to represent the nce sound at the end of a word. The comma is always attached to the preceding letter to avoid confusion with the comma used for punctuation.

chance _c,_ dense _d,_ since _s,_

Notice that you begin the upstroke of the preceding letter before writing the comma. Always loop the *j* and close the small *s* so they will not be mistaken for a comma.

Practice

absence	expense	once
balance	fence	patience
dance	finance	reference
enhance	ignorance	rinse
evidence	influence	sense
excellence	intense	tense

It would not be incorrect to use the comma to represent the nce sound in the middle of a word. However, because it is difficult to write and to transcribe the comma in such a position, it is advisable to use the comma only at the end of a word. For example, the word *dance* is written _d,_ but *dancing* would be written _dnsg_ rather than _d,g_; *intense is* _n,_ but *intensive* would be _ntnsv_ rather than _n,v_.

As was the case under the preceding rule, for some words the sound of the base word is unchanged by the addition of the nce ending. When writing these words, merely add a comma to the Stenoscript for the base word. For example:

appear _ape_ appearance _ape,_

resist _rzS_ resistance _rzS,_

Now write the Stenoscript for these words.

annoyance	clearance	reliance
appliance	defiance	variance

30. Use the small letter x to represent the eeus, shul, and shus sounds. Say the following words to yourself as you write them, so that you will learn to recognize these sounds when you hear them.

a) The eeus sound

courteous kx devious dvx nucleus nkx

Practice

curious	hideous	serious
dubious	mysterious	tedious
envious	obvious	various
glorious	previous	victorious

b) The shul sound

facial fx partial px residential rzdnx

official ofx

Practice

beneficial	financial	racial
credential	influential	social
crucial	judicial	special
essential	potential	superficial

c) The shus sound

anxious agx conscientious kgnx spacious spx

Practice

ambitious	fictitious	pretentious
atrocious	gracious	repetitious
delicious	judicious	suspicious
ferocious	malicious	vicious

REVIEW

I. Words. Write the Stenoscript for the following.

1. tense
2. balance
3. concern
4. appear
5. introduce
6. various
7. entered
8. essential
9. double
10. raise
11. commerce
12. after
13. staff
14. convention
15. suitable
16. legible
17. obvious
18. ambitious
19. proceed
20. commission
21. approximately
22. suspicious
23. dubious
24. chance
25. commercial
26. responsibility
27. instrument
28. capable
29. clearance
30. where
31. even
32. impossible
33. since
34. influence
35. interviewed
36. sentences
37. serious
38. connected
39. chose
40. individuality
41. late
42. blast
43. label
44. social
45. reference
46. crucial
47. whose
48. beginning
49. corporation
50. entrance
51. continue
52. expanse
53. hideous
54. financial
55. their
56. achieve
57. against
58. counterfeit
59. appreciation
60. ever
61. satisfied
62. specification
63. establish
64. spacious
65. any
66. contradict
67. often
68. upon
69. manufacturing
70. never
71. again
72. mistrust

II. Sentences. Write the Stenoscript for the following.

1. The controversy is liable to continue for some time.
2. The consent of city officials is essential to the success of our enterprise.
3. For reasons of national security it is essential that the identity of our informant be concealed.
4. Our organization tries to provide every capable individual with the opportunity to assume a position of responsibility.
5. The evidence indicates that the majority of people are concerned because of the current international situation.

6. No facilities suitable for our purpose are available in this city.
7. The company representative assured us that his organization manufactures appliances of the very finest quality.
8. A special organization has been formed to improve social conditions in our community.
9. We are confident that the social welfare plans will be approved by the special presidential commission.
10. It is difficult but possible to control all of the variable factors in order to remedy the present situation.

III. Paragraphs. Write the Stenoscript for the following.

1.
Dear Madam:

We would be pleased to have your association use our facilities for your meetings. We have special rates for nonprofit organizations and we would make every effort to take care of your particular needs.

I am certain that suitable arrangements can be made, and I would be happy to meet with you at your convenience to discuss this matter further.

Sincerely yours,

2.
Gentlemen:

For various reasons we are considering moving our entire business organization to your city.

Our manufacturing plant would be a spacious one and would require a considerable amount of land. Since we are particularly interested in facilities for efficient shipping of our merchandise, we would appreciate information concerning property for sale in the immediate vicinity of the railroad yard.

Any help that you can give us will be most welcome.

Yours truly,

3.
Dear Mr. Carter:

We have a letter from Miss Carol Morgan applying for an administrative position with our organization. We would like to verify the dates of her attendance at your school and to receive a record of her grades.

Any information regarding her character and dependability will also be appreciated. Since she would be doing some very confidential work, it is essential that we learn all that we can of her background. Any such information will be held in strict confidence.

A stamped self-addressed envelope is enclosed for your convenience in replying. Thank you for your assistance in this matter.

Yours truly,

4.
Dear Sir:

To show our appreciation for your prompt payment for the appliances you purchased a short time ago, we have given you a special discount. It has been credited to your account as shown by the special entry on the enclosed statement.

We hope that you will enjoy the high-quality merchandise you have purchased, and we look forward to serving you in the future.

Sincerely,

5.
Dear Sir:

We are pleased to learn that you are interested in representing our company in dealings with the government. As you know, we have been in the manufacturing business for approximately a century. During that time we have had very satisfactory business relations with the various corporations and government agencies we have dealt with. We feel that our success is due to the high caliber of our personnel as well as to the high quality of our merchandise.

We would therefore appreciate your sending us a complete record of your past employment and any other information that you feel may help us in making our decision. Since the particular job for which you are applying can lead to the position of sales manager, we are looking for a competent, reliable individual with administrative ability as well as merchandising experience.

If you should have any questions concerning your application, do not hesitate to contact us.

Sincerely,

IV. Transcription. Transcribe the following.

wn u r b Nvu f a jb, i i mpt
—l— fs mpj— mpyr hz v u i a
gd wn. // u ape; + psnll l nf, z
opnn v u. u zd b ds n sc a wa
—l— Nvur l fe —l u h gd ls
+ jj— + —l u r ne n evg u d.
a pz— sme + vys l hp l kv, m
v u abll l gl alg w— ppl, prl
w— flo mpye. // rmmbr l h akrl
+ kpe nfo kong— na + ads v
ndv w r qlf + lg l gv u a
rfr,.

Chapter 7

31. Write the small letter *s* when you hear the sub sound.

submit sml   sublet sll

Practice

subject	subscribe	subtract
sublease	subside	subtropical
submarine	substitute	suburb
submission	subtitle	subway

32. Use the small letter *a* to represent the letter group *ad* (pronounced add) at the beginning of a word.

adequate aql   admit aml

Practice

adhere	admiration	admission
admirable	admire	advance

advantage	adverse	advise
adventure	advertise	advocate

In words that begin with *add,* write one *d.* For example,

adding adg addition adj address ads

33. Write the capital letter *C* when you hear the <u>circ</u> and <u>circum</u> sounds.

circle Cl circumvent Cv

Practice

circular	circulation	circumscribe
circulate	circumference	circus

34. Use the small letter *v* to represent the <u>tive</u> letter-group sound.

detective dtkv positive pzv

Practice

comparative	indicative	protective
definitive	inquisitive	relative
formative	lucrative	selective
imperative	prerogative	talkative

35. Write the small letter *l* when you hear the <u>lee</u> sound at the end of a word, and write *Bl* when you hear the <u>blee</u> sound at the end of a word.

rapidly rpdl family fml possibly psBl

annually anll

Practice

capably	locally	probably
easily	luckily	properly
finally	monopoly	secretly
formerly	normally	suddenly
legibly	notably	totally

36. Use the capital letter *F* to represent the sound of *ful* or *fully*. Make the capital *F* by writing a figure seven and crossing it. It is easy to write and readily distinguishable.

full F	careful kaF	watchful wcF
fully F	carefully kaF	watchfully wcF

Practice

faithful	masterfully	thankfully
fearful	needful	trustfully
gainful	neglectfully	wistfully
hopeful	plentifully	wonderful

I. Words. Write the Stenoscript for the following.

1. business
2. capable
3. circumstance
4. compete
5. substance
6. previous
7. descriptive
8. circular
9. attentive
10. orderly
11. consecutive
12. ever
13. believe
14. hope
15. which
16. appearance
17. cost
18. against
19. advise
20. hurry
21. price
22. repetitious
23. immediate
24. again
25. appreciate
26. reference
27. subscription
28. interview
29. opportunity
30. financial
31. executive
32. comparative
33. descriptive
34. silently
35. helpful
36. receive
37. sister
38. capitalist
39. impossible
40. severe
41. position
42. still
43. from
44. accomplish
45. comparatively
46. information
47. representation
48. late
49. represent
50. expense
51. satisfy
52. consent
53. various
54. ambitious
55. incidentally
56. conservative
57. exclusively
58. quarterly
59. careful
60. most
61. piece
62. hopeful
63. after
64. best
65. stand
66. once
67. compel
68. carry
69. annually
70. since
71. raise
72. advocate

II. Sentences. Write the Stenoscript for the following.

1. Their representative suggested that we install a costly substitute for the defective part.
2. We have not previously advertised this admirable product, but we are now advocating a massive sales campaign.
3. The circulation of that newspaper is normally less than ten thousand, but after the terrible crime it approximated fifty thousand, excluding home subscriptions.
4. It is imperative that the information be distributed both locally and nationally, so that the situation can be adequately evaluated by the people before the elections.

5. The detective kept a watchful eye on the subway, hopeful of finally catching the runaway children.
6. The adverse reaction of the public to the protective tax finally provoked a change in policy.
7. Locally, the new candidate was favored, but nationally, he was hopelessly behind.
8. He accomplished the difficult task easily, in fact, masterfully.
9. The beautiful circus performer advanced fearlessly along the rope.
10. Luckily, the subtropical climate is admirably suited to her delicate health.

III. Paragraphs. Write the Stenoscript for the following.

1.
Dear Mr. Smith:

We are happy to inform you that our executive committee has approved your proposal. We will be ready to organize work on your project as soon as a contract has been signed. A tentative rough contract accompanies this letter. Please examine it and let us know if the terms are satisfactory to you. We can then go immediately to a final version.

May I say for myself and all the officers of the company that we appreciate this opportunity to work with a man of your fine reputation on such a worthy project. We are looking forward to an interesting and productive relationship with your group.

Yours very truly,

2.
Gentlemen:

We are writing to remind you of the terms of your contract with us, which calls for satisfactory completion of your work by June 1. We are concerned that you will not meet the terms of the contract, since we have not yet seen your sketches or plans. It is our custom to warn subcontractors if we think they are in danger of defaulting. There are frequently ways in which we can help our suppliers meet their obligations to us.

May we advise you to visit our offices fairly soon, so that we may examine carefully the reasons for the delay and perhaps offer some helpful suggestions. We are prepared to meet with you at your convenience, but it is imperative that it be in the near future.

Very truly yours,

3.
Dear Mr. Smith:

The new samples of carpeting I spoke to you about recently have finally arrived in our showroom. We think they are exactly what you are looking for. They are samples of a carpeting that is especially made for use in stores and offices where traffic is expected to be heavy. You have a discriminating clientele, and we know it is imperative that you be quite selective in your choice of rugs and furnishings. We think our carpeting will meet your high standards of quality in material and design. Please come in, but do let us know in advance so that we will be prepared to serve you.

Sincerely yours,

4.
Dear Sir:

Last May I sent to your order department an order in the amount of $52.53, which was to be shipped to the address shown on the enclosed bill. I subsequently received an acknowledgment of the order with a copy of it enclosed. In June I received a statement from your billing department showing that I still owed the amount of $52.53. I responded by writing and explaining that the payment for the order had been enclosed in my original letter. Since then I have been receiving bills regularly from your billing department, which add interest charges to the original sum. Since my check cleared the bank long ago, I am at a loss to know why you continue to bill me.

Will you please look into this matter carefully with your billing department? I am hopeful that you will resolve this situation soon and submit to me a new statement, showing that my account with you has been paid in full.

Yours very truly,

5.
Dear Mrs. Miller:

Thank you for your recent order for a queen-size bed. It will be delivered as promised.

I am taking this opportunity to enclose a circular describing the bedding that is on sale at this time. You may want to take advantage of this special sale, which we have annually in May. Prices will go back to normal in June, so it is imperative that you act quickly if you would like to have some of this fine bedding at bargain prices. You will probably notice that we include in this sale a queen-size electric blanket. This has been a very popular number with our customers. We have had comparatively few complaints about the service it gives in spite of the fact that we have been carrying these blankets in stock since 1963. The blanket is beautifully bound and comes in five lovely colors.

We are always pleased to serve you in whatever way we can. May we process your order for bedding soon?

Very truly yours,

IV. Transcription. Transcribe the following.

d mmbr: — nkz_ Clr dke — akvl
pgm v — bg lwn h kb, wc u
h jS jyn. w avka — l ec nu
mmbr Ug a kpe fzkl xmnj
bf bg r pgm. — n wn v r h
xp/ l rk a pgm v xsz, Se b,
+ msj kkla l b hpj n bd bdg
+ wa rdkj.// w rk — l u vzl
— h kb rglrl + la avj v r
olmpk sz pu // fnll, w r pz_
l lk u z a mmbr, + hoj — l
u l la 7 avj v r fsll. uvl,

Chapter 8

37. Write the small letter *u* when you hear the un sound at the beginning of a word.

Say the following words as you write them to help you recognize the un sound.

unable *uaB* unofficial *uofx* untimely *utl*

unnecessary *unssy*

Practice

unbend	unfed	unnatural
uncommon	ungracious	unrest
uncut	uninterested	unsafe
uneasy	unless	untidy
unequal	unload	until

38. Write the capital letter *T* when you hear the sound of *trans* at the beginning of a word.

transact *Tak* transcribe *Tkr* transit *Tl*

Practice

transaction	transform	transparent
transcript	transformation	transplant
transcription	translate	transport
transfer	transmit	transportation

39. Write the small letter *w* when you hear the ow sound.

doubt *dwl* how *hw* loud *lwd*

Practice

allow	council	now
aloud	crowd	ounce
arouse	down	voucher
brown	mouth	vowel

Do not, however, write the *w* when the ow sound occurs before the nt or nd sound. For example:

account *ak* found *f*

Now try to write the Stenoscript for these words.

around	endow	mountain
bound	flower	power
couch	foul	renown
counsel	fountain	sound
discount	frown	surround
encounter	lounge	town

40. Memorize the Stenoscript abbreviations for time and direction.

a) Days

Sunday *Sn*	Wednesday *Wd*	Friday *Fr*
Monday *Mn*	Thursday *Th*	Saturday *St*
Tuesday *Ts*		

b) Months

January *Ja*	May *Ma*	September *Sp*
February *Fb*	June *Ju*	October *Oc*
March *Mr*	July *Jl*	November *Nv*
April *Ap*	August *Ag*	December *Dc*

c) Time of day

A.M. *a*	P.M. *p*

d) Direction

north *N*	west *W*	southeast *SE*
south *S*	northeast *NE*	southwest *SW*
east *E*	northwest *NW*	

REVIEW

I. Words. Write the Stenoscript for the following.

1. now
2. unnecessary
3. January
4. June
5. 10 A.M.
6. Tuesday
7. transferred
8. carefully
9. about
10. surrounding
11. approximately
12. untimely
13. March
14. lately
15. northeast
16. Wednesday
17. unlikely
18. August
19. expensive
20. northwest
21. after
22. around
23. opportunity
24. sublet
25. December
26. proud
27. week
28. wonderful
29. July
30. voucher
31. Monday
32. translation
33. somehow
34. April
35. previously
36. Friday
37. disallow
38. apparently
39. 7 P.M.
40. southeast
41. loudly
42. month
43. finally
44. May
45. transparent
46. without
47. recount
48. particular
49. relatively
50. November
51. abundance
52. day
53. circumstance
54. adequate
55. unequaled
56. circular
57. September
58. thankful
59. transportation
60. Saturday
61. transcript
62. substitute
63. announcement
64. February
65. endowment
66. year
67. warehouse
68. October
69. Sunday
70. attentively
71. southwest
72. Thursday

II. Sentences. Write the Stenoscript for the following.

1. On Monday, January 24, we will announce our decision on the awarding of contracts.
2. Most of the people in the crowd came from the surrounding towns.
3. A faulty transmission made the car unsafe for driving.
4. The men hope to finish unloading the merchandise by 3 P.M. on Saturday.
5. Until we have received all of the necessary information, we are unable to complete the transaction.
6. In about two weeks our company will transfer all of our records to our new offices.

7. Because you have seniority, it is unlikely that you will be transferred.
8. Our special excursion rate includes round-trip transportation as well as hotel accommodations for nine days.
9. Unless he encounters unforeseen opposition, he should be able to persuade the town council to accept his proposal.
10. Public transportation on the south side of the city is unreliable.

III. Paragraphs. Write the Stenoscript for the following.

1.
Dear Mr. Brown:

Thank you for your letter of October 14. We did make a mistake on the transportation charges and we appreciate your calling this error to our attention.

Our records have been adjusted and your account now shows a credit of $17.

Sincerely,

2.

Dear Mrs. Cowley:

We have received your letter of December 3 in which you advised us that the couch and chairs you received last week arrived in damaged condition. We notified the express company of this situation and they admitted that the furniture was damaged in transit.

Rest assured that the damaged pieces will be replaced without any cost to you. We would, however, appreciate more information about the condition of the furniture so that we may file our claim for damage.

Thank you for your assistance in this matter.

Very truly yours,

3.
Dear Sir:

Enclosed is your statement showing an unpaid balance of $306.00. This figure includes the transactions of January 5 and March 10. During the past year we have made many allowances for unfortunate circumstances that prevented prompt payment of this bill. However, since we have received no payment and have had no word from you in the past month, we are quite concerned.

Unless we hear from you within the week, we will be forced to turn this matter over to our lawyers.

Yours truly,

4.
Dear Bill,

The annual meeting for company salesmen in Boston and the surrounding area will be held February 11, 12, and 13 at the Atlas Hotel in Boston.

Because these days will be very busy ones, all meals will be served in the hotel dining room. You will be asked to select your menus in advance to avoid any unnecessary delay in food service.

Arrangements for food, transportation, and room reservations are being handled by Mary Towner. You should be hearing from her within the next few days.

We are all looking forward to seeing you here next month.

Sincerely,

5.
Dear Sir:

We regret to inform you that the Powers Hotel is unable to reserve a room for you on Saturday and Sunday, May 1 and 2.

We will be more than happy to attempt to make reservations in another hotel. However, owing to the presence of two large conventions in the city on those days, it is unlikely that suitable accommodations will be available. We suggest that, if at all possible, you postpone your visit until the following week, when the hotels will be less crowded.

Since all travel arrangements depend on the dates of your trip, we are anxious to hear from you about this matter.

Yours truly,

IV. Transcription. Transcribe the following.

ds: m co r h lB Jp9 — r mds
rpdl l sml lwn. w v Nmdl
lkg co h ma a spx Sd v — s

pbm. —u arny— w— m sml b

rliB lkg co, w r nw aB l gv

Vm svs l ne lwn w—n 300 mi v

— sl. ull —s pn z w— O b

s, i lk svrl D l ma dlvy l sm

v —z lwn. // w—g u l li —s

nu svs. pz kl o s l hp u —nx

li u h a zp—g l ne lwn wa

svs hz b so n — pS. ul,

Summary of Rules for Stenoscript® ABC Shorthand

1. Write vowel sounds at the beginning or end of a word. Do not write vowel sounds within a word.
2. When the initial or final sound of a word is the name of a letter of the alphabet, write that letter.
3. When a base word ends in a double consonant sound, write the first of the two sounds. (Other rules involving consonants take precedence over this rule.)
4. Whenever *d* or *ed* is added to a base word, underline the last letter or symbol.
5. A plural word ending in *s* or *es* is written the same as the singular form.
6. Use regular punctuation. Do not use the hyphen. Use two slant marks to indicate a new paragraph.
7. You may use any common abbreviation that is shorter than the Stenoscript form. Write figures for numbers except *one,* which is written *wn.* However, very large rounded numbers, such as *million* and *billion,* are treated as words.

8. Memorize the Stenoscript forms on the High-Frequency Word List.
9. Write the small letter c when you hear the ch sound of *chop.*
10. Use a dash to represent the word *the* and the sounds of *th, nd, nt, mand, mend,* and *ment.*
11. Write the small letter g when you hear the ng sound as in *angle* and *eating.*
12. Write the small letter *j* when you hear the shun, chun, or zhun sound as in *action, question,* and *occasion.*
13. Write the small letter z when you hear the sh or zh sound as in *fish* and *measure.*
14. Use the small letter *q* to represent the nk sound, as in *bank,* and the qu letter-group sound, as in *quit.*
15. Do not write an *l* if the l sound occurs **within** a base word and is preceded or followed by a different consonant sound.
16. Do not write an *r* if the r sound occurs **within** a base word and is preceded or followed by a different consonant sound.

17. Use a slant mark to represent the sounds of *rd, rt,* and *rk* and the letter group *ward.*

18. Use the small letter *y* to represent the *ry* and *rry* letter groups (pronounced ree) at the end of words, and the oi sound of *annoy.*

19. Write the small letter *m* when you hear the sound of *mis* or *im* at the beginning of a word.

20. Write the small letter *d* when you hear the dis or des sound at the beginning of a word.

21. Use special abbreviations for the salutation and the complimentary close of a letter.

22. When the final single consonant sound of a base word is preceded by a long-vowel sound, **write the vowel sound** when you write the word, but **drop** the final consonant sound. However, when the final consonant is a j sound, v sound, or z sound, write these sounds instead of the long-vowel sound.

23. **Write the vowel sound** but **drop** the *r* when you write words that end in the following letter-group sounds: ar as in *fair,* er as in *here,* or as in *roar,* and ur as in *poor.*

24. Write the capital letter *S* when you hear the st letter-group sound. 65

25. Memorize the 24 brief forms.

26. Write the small letter *k* when you hear the sound of *com, con,* or *counter* at the beginning of a word.

27. Write the capital letter *N* when you hear the sound of *enter, entr, inter,* or *intr* at the beginning of a word.

28. Write the capital letter *B* when you hear the ble sound at the end of a word, as in *able.*

29. Use a comma to represent the nce sound at the end of a word, as in *chance.*

30. Use the small letter *x* to represent the eeus, shul, and shus sounds, as in *devious, facial,* and *spacious.*

31. Write the small letter *s* when you hear the sub sound of *submit.*

32. Use the small letter *a* to represent the letter group *ad* (pronounced add) at the beginning of a word.

33. Write the capital letter *C* when you hear the circ and circum sounds, as in *circle* and *circumvent.*

34. Use the small letter *v* to represent the tive letter-group sound, as in *positive.*

35. Write the small letter *l* when you hear the lee sound at the end of a word, as in *rapidly*, and write *Bl* when you hear the blee sound at the end of a word, as in *possibly.*

36. Use the capital letter *F* to represent the sound of *ful* or *fully.*

37. Write the small letter *u* when you hear the un sound at the beginning of a word, as in *unable* and *unnecessary.*

38. Write the capital letter *T* when you hear the sound of *trans* at the beginning of a word.

39. Write the small letter *w* when you hear the ow sound of *how.*

40. Memorize the Stenoscript abbreviations for time and direction.

Using Stenoscript® ABC Shorthand

Now that you have mastered the theory of Stenoscript, you should attempt to build up your skill at taking dictation. This chapter will give you some practical advice on how to take dictation, how to transcribe your notes more quickly, and how to use shorthand in notetaking and will offer other helpful suggestions on how to make Stenoscript a useful tool for you.

Taking Dictation

You must practice taking dictation every day. This is extremely important, because it is the only means of attaining your speed goal.

You must continuously attempt to take dictation at a speed somewhat higher than your ability. When you are able to take dictation at a given speed with only three to five errors, you should increase the dictation speed 10 words a minute. Gradually you will improve your ability to coordinate what you hear with what you write.

It is best to take shorthand from a person experienced in giving dictation or from timed records or tapes. You will find that an inexperienced person will not dictate evenly or accurately. He may even find himself pacing you because it will be tempting for him not to leave you behind. Rather, he should challenge you by increasing his speed as you progress.

Your first speed goal should be 60 words a minute. The average person writes longhand at approximately 40 words a minute. At the beginning, as you attempt to put Stenoscript theory into practice, you will find that you probably cannot take the dictation at 60 words a minute. Nevertheless, after five or ten one-minute speed tests, you will begin to gain both accuracy and speed. When you attain the speed of 60 words a minute and are making only three to five errors, you should set your goal at 70 words a minute and thereafter increase it each time you master a new speed level.

The aim of all shorthand systems is to reduce your writing to a minimum and to increase your ability to write more words a minute. With regular practice and constant use, many Stenoscript students are able to take dictation at the rate of 100 or even 120 words a minute.

Time yourself, using a stopwatch or an ordinary clock with a second hand. It is important that you keep accurate time so that you know your exact speed.

Write as quickly as you can and be as accurate as possible. Omit words that are difficult for you. You will learn these words in time. Concentration on a single word during dictation could cause you to lose an entire sentence.

After each speed test, have the person giving the dictation read the material slowly so that you can correct any errors in your shorthand. This is important.

Letters and paragraphs in most dictation books are divided into groups of 20 words. Use the table below to determine correct dictation speed.

Number of Words a Minute	Dictating Time for Each Group of 20 Words
40	30 seconds
50	24 seconds
60	20 seconds
70	17 seconds
80	15 seconds
90	13 seconds
100	12 seconds
110	11 seconds
120	10 seconds

Adapting Stenoscript to Your Job

Shorthand courses do not prepare you to use special or technical business vocabularies, but Stenoscript can be adapted to your particular job.

You have learned that in Stenoscript certain capital letters represent specific words. The remaining capital letters can be used for those words that occur most frequently in your business communications. For example, in insurance transactions you could represent the word *liability,* a commonly used insurance term, with the capital letter *L*.

The following capital letters can be used for special business terms:

A, B, C, G, H, J, K, L, P, Q, R, T, X, Z.

Transcribing Stenoscript

Of all shorthand systems, Stenoscript is probably the easiest to transcribe, and you should have no difficulty with it. Remember the following points, however; they will help you transcribe your notes more rapidly.

Vowels are written only at the beginning or end of a Stenoscript form of a base word. So when you see a vowel written within a word, you know that the vowel begins or ends a base word to which a prefix or suffix has been added. For example, *r, d, u,* or *T* before a vowel could stand respectively for the prefix *re, dis, un,* or *trans; B, g, l, r,* or *v* after a vowel could represent the suffix *able, ing, ly, er,* or *tive.* **Transcribe the base word first and then add the prefix or suffix.**

Now look at the following examples.

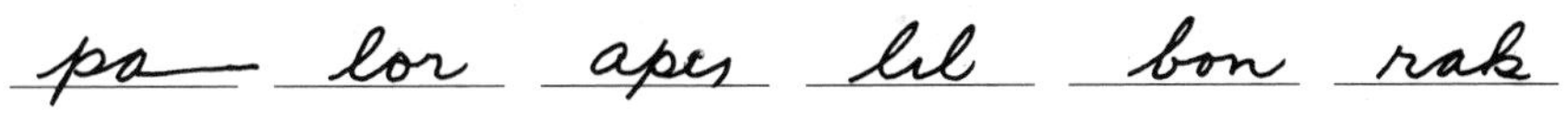

In the first example, if you transcribe only as far as *pa,* you have the base word *pay.* By adding the suffix represented by the dash, you have the word *payment.* The second word transcribed through *lo* gives you the base word *low,* and adding the suffix *r* gives you *lower.* Transcribing the other words, you first get *apply,* then *appliance; like,* then *likely; broke,* then *broken.* In the last example, you transcribe the base word *act* and add the prefix *re* to get the word *react.*

As you have learned, there are two kinds of words whose Stenoscript form ends in a vowel: words that end in a vowel sound (*pay, low*); and words in which the final single consonant sound is preceded by a long-vowel sound (*broke, like*). The chart below lists possible final consonants for words to which the long-vowel rule applies. It will help you transcribe words in the second category quickly and accurately. For example, if you could not transcribe the word *fe* as *fee* in the following sentence, you would go to the chart and find that by adding a single consonant sound at the end you could form *feed, feel, fear, feat, feet, free, flee,* or *fleet.* (Don't forget about an *l* or *r* that might have dropped out.)

— by dz n fe l.

Looking at the word in the context of the sentence, however, would tell you that *fe* must logically be *feel.* The sentence reads: *The boy does not feel well.*

Now transcribe the following sentence:

I l rma af evrwn g.

The chart will show you that possible transcriptions for *rma* are *remain, remake,* and *remade.* From the context of the sentence you would immediately know that the word must be *remain.* The transcription reads: *I will remain after everyone goes.*

Remember that this chart lists the consonant **sound** and **not the spelling** of the word ending. One sound may have several spellings. For example, the sound of ā plus *d* may be spelled *ade* as in *made* or *aid* as in *maid.* When transcribing a difficult word, try adding each consonant sound to the final long vowel of the word and then try the word in the context of the sentence. Remember that you pronounce the *a* as in *pay,* the e as in *fee,* the *i* as in *pie,* the o as in *show,* and the *u* as in *shoe* or *cue.*

Here is the list of possible single consonant ending sounds.

- *b*
- c (as in ace)
- *d*
- *f*
- g (as in *vogue,* but not as in cage)
- *k*
- *l*
- *m*
- *n*
- *p*
- *q* (as in *antique*)
- *r* (with a as in *care,* e as in *fear,* o as in *more, u* as in *poor*)
- *s* (as in case, but not as in *tease*)
- *t*

Connecting the words of commonly used phrases will increase the speed of experienced shorthand writers. After you have mastered the theory of Stenoscript and learned to take dictation accurately, you will find phrasing valuable for writing familiar, frequently used groups of words.

Phrasing follows the standard Stenoscript forms except that the words in the phrase are connected. For example, the phrase *Thank you for your letter* would be written

—qufullr

Phrasing is a skill that can be attained only after diligent practice, but is almost limitless in its application.

The following are some frequently used business phrases and their Stenoscript forms.

about the	ag—	at any	lne
all of them	lvm	at any time	lnele
are not	rn	at once	lwn
as good as	zgdz	at that	l l
as great as	zgaz	did not	dn
as low as	zloz	does not	dzn
as many as	zmz	for the	f—
as much as	zmcz	for us	fs
as to	zl	from the	fm—
as you	zu	from you	fmu
as well as	zlz	from your	fmu
at all	ll	have been able	hbaB

he is	ei
he had	eh
he was not	ezn
he will	el
I do not	Idn
I do not believe	Idnblv
I do not know	Idnn
I do not see	Idnc
I had	Ih
I have	Ih
if you are	iur
if you will	iul
if the	i—
in due course	ndks
in due time	ndti
in his	nz
in reply	nrpi
in which	nwc
into the	nt—
is not	in
it may be	imab
it is not	iin
it must be	imSb
it was not	izn
more than	mo—n
must be	mSb
of it	vi
of its	vi
of their	v—r
of them	v—m
of these	v—z
of this	v—s
of which	vwc
on our	or
on the	o—
on you	ou
on your	ou
over the	V—
should be	zdb
should be able	zdbaB
that is	—li
that they	—la
that this	—ls
there are	—rr

there is	—ri	to place	lpa
there is not	—rin	to say	lsa
they do not	—adn	to see	lc
they do not know	—adnn	to ship	lzp
they had	—ah	to take	lla
through the	—u	to this	l—s
to ask	las	to which	lwc
to be	lb	to work	lw/
to draw	lda	was not	zn
to get	lgl	we are	wr
to give	lgv	we are not	wrn
to go	lg	we can	wk
to honor	lonr	we do not	wdn
to keep	lke	we do not believe	wdnblv
to know	ln	we had	wh
to make	lma	we have	wh
to me	le	we have been	whb
to mean	lme	we have not	whn
to meet	lme	we may	wma
to my	lm	we must	wm&
to our	lr	we shall	wzl
to pay	lpa	we shall be	wzlb

we shall not	wzln
we should	wzd
we will	wl
we will not	wln
we would	wwd
what to do	wlld
when the	wn—
which have	wch
which is	wcs
who have	wh
will be able	lbaB
will you	lu
with us	w—s
with that	w—l
with the	w—
would be able	wdbaB
you are	ur
you do not	udn
you do not know	udnn
you had	uh
you have	uh
you know	un
your letter	ullr
you may	uma
you would	uwd

Notetaking in Stenoscript

Stenoscript is invaluable for notetaking as well as for taking dictation. Whether you are taking notes in the classroom, at a lecture, or at a meeting, it is essential that you have an efficient notetaking technique. By observing the basic principles presented here, you can improve the quality of your notes.

1. **Listen carefully.** This is the first step in effective notetaking. To take meaningful notes, you must understand what is being said. If your notes are solely for your own use, wait until a speaker has expressed a complete thought and then summarize it in your own words.

At other times it will be important to note exactly what has been said. In the classroom, for example, the teacher may indicate that a particular statement should be copied word for word. When your notes are to be used for an official purpose—for the minutes of a meeting, for example—record the speaker's phrases rather than your own summary. Unless it is essential that a statement be recorded verbatim, do not worry about taking down every word or about using complete sentences. In fact, you will find that when material is being presented in a very orderly fashion, a simple topic outline (word or phrase) may be best suited to your needs.

2. **Take down only the main points and the important details of the material presented.** Look for verbal clues to help you recognize the important points. Phrases such as *In the first place, I would like to call your attention to . . .,* and *In conclusion* indicate that the statements that follow may be worth noting.

3. **Edit your notes.** Reread them while the material is still fresh in your mind. You will then be able to rewrite any carelessly formed words and write the long form for those abbreviated words that later might prove difficult to read. You may also wish to underline key ideas, add or eliminate certain details, or completely reorganize your notes. (This would be particularly true for notes taken at a meeting when no definite agenda had been followed, for class notes when there had been a great deal of discussion, or for lecture notes when the material had not been presented in an organized manner.)

In addition to these basic principles there are several practical hints that will help you take more efficient notes.

Be sure that you have the necessary materials. A ballpoint pen is preferable to a pencil. The point will not break or wear down and you can save time by crossing out errors rather than erasing them. Be sure to have several pens in case one runs out of ink.

Check to see that you have enough paper in your stenopad or notebook. Overestimate your needs to be on the safe side.

Use a firm surface to write on—if not a table, then a clipboard or the hard cover of a notebook.

Decide on a means of identifying the topic, and place this identification at the top of each page of your notes. Notes for a biology class might have "Bio" written at the top of the page. "PR2" could key note pages for the second in a series of public relations meetings. Dating and numbering your pages will be an additional means of identification if one page becomes separated from the others. Identifying can be done either before or after the actual notetaking; do not waste time labeling pages when you should be concentrating on what is being said.

Whenever possible, try to find out in advance the topic or topics to be discussed. Then devise your own Stenoscript abbreviations for certain words—

names and special terms—that you know will be mentioned frequently. For example, if you are attending a conference on the training of unskilled workers, you might use abbreviations similar to the following: *Uw* for *unskilled worker; T* for *train; FG* for *federal government; Pn* for *private industry.*

If you are taking notes at a meeting where it is important to record the names of the speakers, try to obtain a list of participants beforehand and learn who they are so that you can identify them during the meeting. Devise special Stenoscript abbreviations for their names and a system to indicate when they are speaking.

A good way to practice and to build up your skill is to take notes while listening to panel discussions, lectures, and interview programs on radio or television.

These are only a few of the ways to improve your notetaking skills. As you become more experienced, you will discover your own shortcuts for more efficient and accurate notetaking.

Stenoscript® ABC Shorthand
Business Word List

STENOSCRIPT® ABC SHORTHAND BUSINESS WORD LIST*

A

a	a
a.m.	a
abandon	ab—n
abbreviation	abvj
ability	abll
able	aB
abnormal	abnml
aboard	ab/
abolish	ablz
about	ao
above	abv
abrupt	abp
absence	abs,
absent	abs—
absolute	abslu
absolutely	abslul
absorb	absb
absorbent	absb—
abstract	abSk
abundance	ab—,
abundant	ab—
abuse (*n.*)	abu
abuse (*vb.*)	abz
academic	akdmk
academy	akdme
accelerate	akslra
acceleration	akslj
accent	aks—
accept	aksp
acceptable	akspB
acceptance	aksp,
accepting	akspg
access	akss
accessory	akssy
accident	aksd—
accidental	aksd—l
accommodate	akmda
accommodation	akmdj
accompaniment	ac
accompanist	ac
accompany	ac
accompanying	ac
accomplish	ac
accomplishing	ac
accomplishment	ac
accord	ak/
accordance	ak/,
according	ak/g

*Abbreviations used: *adj.*, adjective; *n.*, noun; *u.m.*, unit modifier; *vb.*, verb.

accost	akS
account	ak—
accountant	ak——
accounting	ak—g
accredit	akdl
accrue	aku
accumulate	akmla
accuracy	akrc
accurate	akrl
accuse	akz
accustom	akSm
achieve	acv
achievement	acv—
acid	asd
acknowledge	ak
acknowledging	ak
acknowledgment	ak
acquaint	aq—
acquire	aqi
acquisition	aqzz
acquit	aql
acre	akr
acreage	akrj
across	aks
act	ak
action	akj
active	akv
activity	akvl
actual	akcl
adaptable	adpB
add	ad
adding	adg
addition	adj
additional	adjl
address	ads
addressee	adse
adequate	aql
adequately	aqll
adhere	ahe
adhesive	ahsv
adjacent	ajs—
adjudge	ajj
adjust	ajS
adjustable	ajSB
adjusting	ajSg
adjustment	ajS—
administer	adm
administering	adm
administrate	adm
administration	adm
administrative	adm
administrator	adm
admirable	amrB
admiration	amrj
admire	ami
admission	amj
admit	aml
admittance	aml,

adopt	adp
adoption	adpj
adult	adl
advance	avn
advancement	avn—
advantage	avj
adventure	avncr
adverse	avs
advertise	av z
advertisement	av z—
advertiser	av zr
advertising	av zg
advice	avs
advisable	avzB
advise	avz
adviser	avzr
advising	avzg
advisory	avzy
advocate (*n.*)	avkl
advocate (*vb.*)	avka
advocating	avkag
affair	afa
affect	afk
affecting	afkg
affection	afkj
affidavit	afdvl
affiliate (*n.*)	afll
affiliate (*vb.*)	afla
affiliation	aflj
afford	af
afraid	afa
after	af
afternoon	afnu
afterthought	afl
again	ag
against	ag
age	aj
agency	ajnc
agent	aj—
aggregate (*n.*)	aggl
aggregate (*vb.*)	agga
aggression	agj
aggressive	agsv
agitate	ajla
agitation	ajlj
agitator	ajlar
ago	ag
agree	age
agreeable	ageB
agreeably	ageBl
agreement	age—
agriculture	agkcr
ahead	ahd
aid	ad
aide	ad
ailment	al—
aim	am
air	ar

air-condition	arkdj
aircraft	arkf
airline	arli
airmail	arma
airplane	arpa
airport	arp/
alarm	alm
album	abm
alcohol	akhl
alert	al/
align	ali
alignment	ali—
alike	ali
alive	alv
all	l
alley	ale
alliance	ali,
allied	ali
allocate	alka
allocation	alkj
allot	all
allotment	all—
allow	alw
allowable	alwB
allowance	alw,
allowing	alwg
alloy	aly
almost	lm$
alone	alo
along	alg
aloof	alu
aloud	alwd
already	lrd
also	lo
alter	alr
alteration	alrj
alternate (*n.*)	alnt
alternate (*vb.*)	alna
alternative	alnv
although	l—o
altogether	ltg—r
aluminum	almnm
always	lwz
am	m
amaze	amz
amazing	amzg
amazingly	amzgl
ambassador	ambsdr
ambition	ambj
ambitious	ambx
ambulance	ambl,
amend	a—
amendment	a— —
amenities	amnt
American	amrkn
ammunition	amnj
among	amg
amortize	am/z

amount	am—	another	an—r
amounting	am—g	answer	ansr
ample	ampl	answering	ansrg
amply	ampl	anticipate	a—spa
amuse	amz	anticipation	a—spj
amusement	amz—	antique	a—e
an	a	antitrust	a—tS
analysis	anlss	anxious	agx
analyst	anlS	any	ne
analyze	anlz	anybody	nebd
ancient	anz—	anyhow	nehw
and	+	anyone	newn
anesthetic	ans—lk	anything	ne—g
angel	anjl	anytime	neti
anger	agr	anyway	newa
angle	agl	anywhere	newa
angry	agy	apart	ap/
animal	anml	apartment	ap/—
annex	anx	apparel	aprl
anniversary	anvsy	apparent	apr—
announce	anw,	apparently	apr—l
announcement	anwns—	appeal	ape
announcing	anwnsg	appear	ape
annoy	any	appearance	ape,
annoyance	any,	appearing	apeg
annual	anl	appease	apz
annually	anll	appendix	ap—x
annuity	anl	appetite	apti
annum	anm	applause	apz

apple	apl	architect	rklk
appliance	ap,	architectural	rklkcrl
applicable	apkB	architecture	rklkcr
applicant	apk—	are	r
application	apkj	area	ara
apply	api	argue	rgu
applying	apig	argument	rgu—
appoint	apy—	arise	arz
appointment	apy—	arm	rm
appraisal	apzl	army	rme
appraise	apz	around	ar—
appreciate	ap	arouse	arwz
appreciating	ap	arrange	arnj
appreciation	ap	arrangement	arnj—
appreciative	ap	arranging	arnjg
apprehension	aphnj	array	ara
approach	apc	arrest	ar$
appropriate (*adj.*)	appl	arrival	arvl
appropriate (*vb.*)	appa	arrive	arv
appropriation	appj	arriving	arvg
approval	apvl	art	/
approve	apv	article	/kl
approximate	apx	artificial	/fx
approximately	apx	artist	/$
approximating	apx	as	z
approximation	apx	aside	asi
April	Ap	ask	as
arbitration	rbj	asking	asg
arch	rc	aspect	aspk

assemble	asmB
assembly	asmBl
assert	as/
assess	ass
assessment	ass—
asset	asl
assign	asi
assignment	asi—
assist	asS
assistance	asS,
assistant	asS—
assisting	asSg
associate	as
associating	as
association	as
assortment	as/—
assume	asu
assumption	asmj
assurance	azu,
assure	azu
assuring	azug
astonish	aSnz
astound	aS—
at	l
ate	al
athletic	a—lk
atlas	als
atmosphere	almsfe
atomic	almk
atrocious	alx
attach	alc
attaching	alcg
attachment	alc—
attack	alk
attain	ala
attempt	almp
attempting	almpg
attend	al—
attendance	al—,
attendant	al——
attending	al—g
attention	alnj
attentive	alnv
attentively	alnvl
attic	alk
attire	ali
attitude	allu
attorney	alne
attract	alk
attraction	alkj
attractive	alkv
attribute	albu
auction	akj
audible	adB
audience	ad,
audit	adl
auditing	adlg
auditor	adlr

auditorium	adlrm	avail	ava
August	Ag	availability	avablt
authentic	a—k	available	avaB
author	a—r	avenue	avnu
authority	a—rt	average	avrj
authorization	a—rzj	aviation	avj
authorize	a—rz	avoid	avyd
auto	alo	await	awa
automatic	almtk	awaiting	awag
automatically	almtkl	award	a/
automation	almj	awarding	a/g
automobile	almbe	aware	awa
automotive	almv	away	awa
autumn	alm	awful	af
auxiliary	agzly	awhile	awl

B

baby	bb	bait	ba
back	bk	bake	ba
background	bkg—	bakery	bay
backing	bkg	balance	bl,
backward	bk/	balcony	bkne
bad	bd	bale	ba
badge	bj	ball	bl
badly	bdl	ballot	blt
bag	bg	ban	bn
baggage	bgj	band	b—
bail	ba	banish	bnz

bank	bq
banker	bqr
banking	bqg
banner	bnr
banquet	bqql
bar	br
barbecue	bbq
barber	bbr
bare	ba
barely	bal
bargain	bgn
barrage	bry
barrel	brl
barricade	brka
barrier	brr
base	ba
baseboard	bab
basement	ba—
basic	bsk
basis	bss
basket	bskl
bath	b—
battery	bly
battle	bll
bay	ba
be	b
beach	bc
bean	be
bear	ba
beard	b/
bearing	bag
beat	be
beaten	ben
beautiful	blf
beautifully	blf
beauty	bl
beaver	bvr
became	bk
because	bkz
become	bk
becoming	bk
bed	bd
bedding	bdg
bedroom	bdru
beef	be
been	b
beetle	bll
before	bf
beg	bg
began	bg
begin	bg
beginner	bgr
beginning	bg
begun	bg
behalf	bhf
behave	bhv
behavior	bhvr
behind	bh—

being	b	bigger	bgr
belief	ble	biggest	bgS
believe	blv	bill	bl
believer	blvr	billing	blg
bell	bl	billion	bln
belong	blg	bin	bn
below	blo	bind	b—
belt	bl	binder	b—r
bench	bnc	binding	b—g
bend	b—	binoculars	bnklr
beneath	bn—	bird	b
beneficial	bnfx	birth	b—
beneficiary	bnfzy	birthday	b—D
benefit	bnfl	birthplace	b—pa
bent	b—	biscuit	bskl
berry	by	bit	bl
beside	bsi	bite	bi
best	bS	bitten	bln
bet	bl	bitter	blr
betray	bla	black	bk
better	blr	blade	ba
between	blwe	blame	ba
beverage	bvrj	blank	bg
beyond	b—	blanket	bgl
Bible	bB	blare	ba
bicycle	bskl	blast	bS
bid	bd	blaze	bz
bidder	bdr	blend	b—
big	bg	bless	bs

blew	bu
blind	b—
blindness	bns
bloc	bk
block	bk
blood	bd
bloom	bu
blossom	bsm
blot	bl
blotter	blr
blow	bo
blue	bu
boar	bo
board	b/
boarding	b/g
boat	bo
body	bd
bold	bd
bolt	bl
bomb	bm
bond	b—
bonding	b—g
bone	bo
bonus	bns
book	bk
bookkeeper	bkker
bookkeeping	bkkeg
booklet	bkll
bookstore	bkSo

boom	bu
boost	bS
boot	bu
booth	b—
border	b—r
bore	bo
boredom	bodm
born	bn
borrow	bro
boss	bs
both	b—
bother	b—r
bottle	bll
bottling	bllg
bottom	blm
bought	bl
boulevard	blv/
bound	b—
boundary	b—y
bouquet	bk
bout	bwl
bowl	bo
box	bx
boxing	bxg
boy	by
brace	ba
bracket	bkl
brake	ba
branch	bnc

brand	b—
brass	bs
brave	bv
bread	bd
break	ba
breakfast	bkfs
breath	b—
breathe	b—
bred	bd
breed	be
breeze	bz
bribe	bi
bribery	biy
brick	bk
bridal	bil
bride	bi
bridegroom	bigu
bridge	bj
brief	be
briefly	bel
bright	bi
brilliant	bl—
bring	bg
bringing	bgg
broad	bd
broadcast	bdks
brochure	bzu
broke	bo
broken	bon
broker	bkr
brokerage	bkrj
bronze	bnz
broom	bu
brother	b—r
brought	bl
brow	bw
brown	bwn
brush	bz
budget	bjl
buff	bf
build	bd
builder	bdr
building	bdg
built	bl
bulb	bb
bulletin	blln
bump	bm
bumper	bmr
bunch	bnc
bundle	b—l
burden	b—n
bureau	bro
burial	brl
burn	bn
bury	by
bus	bs
bushel	bzl
business	bz

businessman	bzmn	button	bln
busy	bz	buy	b
but	b	buying	bg
butane	bla	by	b
butcher	bcr	bylaw	bla
butter	blr	bypass	bps

C

cab	kb	camp	km
cabin	kbn	campaign	kmpa
cabinet	kbnl	campus	kmps
cable	kB	can	k
café	kfa	cancel	knsl
cafeteria	kflra	canceling	knslg
cage	kj	cancellation	knslj
calamity	klml	cancer	knsr
calculate	kkla	candidate	k_da
calculating	kklag	candle	k_l
calculator	kklar	candy	knd
calendar	kl_r	cane	ka
caliber	klbr	cannot	kn
call	kl	canvas	knvs
calling	klg	canvass	knvs
calm	km	cap	kp
calorie	klre	capability	kpbll
came	k	capable	kpB
camera	kmra	capably	kpBl
camouflage	kmfj	capacity	kpsl

capital	kpll	carrot	krl
capitalist	kplls	carry	ky
capitol	kpll	carrying	kyg
capsule	kpsl	carton	k^n
captain	kpln	carve	kv
caption	kpj	case	ka
captive	kpv	cash	kz
capture	kpcr	cashier	kze
car	kr	casket	kskl
carbon	kbn	cast	ks
carbonated	kbn_a_	casual	kzl
card	k/	casualty	kzll
care	ka	cat	kl
career	kre	catalog	kllg
carefree	kafe	catastrophe	klsfe
careful	kaf	catch	kc
carefully	kaf	catching	kcg
careless	kals	category	klgy
carelessness	kalsns	cater	klr
caress	krs	cathedral	k—dl
cargo	kgo	cattle	kll
carload	krlo	caught	kl
carnival	knvl	cause	kz
carol	krl	caution	kj
carpenter	kp—r	cautious	kx
carpet	kpl	cave	kv
carpeting	kplg	cease	se
carriage	kry	cedar	cdr
carrier	kyr	ceiling	clg

celebrate	slba
celebrity	slbl
cell	sl
cellar	slr
cellophane	slfa
cement	s—
cemetery	smly
censor	snsr
cent	s—
center	s—r
central	s—l
century	sncy
ceramic	srmk
ceremony	srmne
certain	s/n
certainly	s/nl
certificate	s/fkl
certification	s/fkj
certify	s/fi
certifying	s/fig
chain	ca
chair	ca
chairman	camn
challenge	clnj
chamber	cmbr
champagne	zmpa
champion	cmpn
chance	c,
change	cnj
changeable	cnjB
channel	cnl
chapter	cplr
character	krklr
characteristic	krklrSk
charge	cj
charitable	crlB
charity	crl
chart	c/
charter	c/r
chattel	cll
chauffeur	zfr
cheap	ce
cheaper	cer
check	ck
checker	ckr
checking	ckg
checkup	ckp
cheer	ce
cheerful	cef
cheese	cz
chemical	kmkl
cherish	crz
cherry	cy
chest	cS
chew	cu
chicken	ckn
chief	ce
child	cd

childhood	cdhd
children	cdn
chill	cl
chimney	cmne
china	cna
chip	cp
chocolate	cklt
choice	cys
choir	kwr
choose	cz
chop	cp
chopping	cpg
chore	co
chorus	krs
chose	cz
chosen	czn
Christmas	ksms
chrome	ko
chronic	knk
church	cc
cider	sdr
cigar	sgr
cigarette	sgrt
cipher	sfr
circle	Cl
circuit	Ct
circular	Clr
circulate	Cla
circulation	Clj
circumference	Cfr,
circumflex	Cfx
circumscribe	Cskb
circumspect	Cspk
circumstance	CS,
circumvent	Cv-
circus	Cs
cite	st
citizen	stzn
citrus	sts
city	st
civic	svk
civil	svl
civilian	svln
civilization	svlzj
claim	ka
clarification	krfkj
clarify	krfi
class	ks
classic	ksk
classification	ksfkj
classify	ksfi
classroom	ksru
clay	ka
clean	ke
cleaner	ker
cleanest	keS
cleaning	keg
clear	ke

clearance	ke,
clearly	kel
clergy	kg
clerical	krkl
clerk	k/
clever	kvr
client	k—
clientele	k—l
climate	kmt
climb	ki
clinic	knk
clinical	knkl
clip	kp
cloak	ko
clock	kk
close (*adj.*)	ko
close (*vb.*)	kz
closely	kol
closet	kzt
closing	kzg
cloth	k—
clothes	kz
clothing	k—g
cloud	kwd
cloudy	kwd
club	kb
clubroom	kbru
clue	ku
cluster	kSr
clutch	kc
coach	kc
coal	ko
coarse	ks
coast	kS
coat	ko
code	ko
coffee	kfe
coil	kyl
coin	kyn
coincidence	knsd,
cold	kd
collapse	klps
collar	klr
collateral	kllrl
collect	klk
collecting	klkg
collection	klky
collective	klkv
collector	klkr
college	klj
collide	kli
collision	klj
color	klr
colorful	klrf
column	klm
columnist	klmS
comb	ko
combat	kbt

combination	kbnj	communication	kmnkj
combine	kbi	communism	kmnzm
combustion	kbsj	communist	kmnS
come	k	community	kmnl
comedy	kd	commuter	kmur
comfort	kf	compact	kpk
comfortable	kfB	companion	kpnn
coming	k	company	co
command	k—	comparable	kprB
commander	k—r	comparative	kpav
commanding	k—g	comparatively	kpavl
commence	km,	compare	kpa
commencement	kmns—	comparing	kpag
commendation	k—j	comparison	kpasn
comment	k—	compartment	kp—
commentator	k—ar	compass	kps
commerce	kms	compatible	kplB
commercial	kmx	compel	kpl
commission	kmj	compensation	kpnsj
commissioner	kmjr	compete	kpe
commit	kml	competence	kpl,
commitment	kml—	competent	kpl—
committee	kml	competing	kpeg
commodity	kmdl	competition	kplj
common	kmn	competitive	kplv
commonly	kmnl	compilation	kplj
commonwealth	kmnw—	compile	kpi
commotion	kmj	complain	kpa
communicate	kmnka	complaint	kp—

complete	kpe	concentrate	ks—a
completely	kpel	concept	ksp
completing	kpeg	conception	kspj
completion	kpj	concern	ksn
complex	kpx	concerning	ksng
complexion	kpkj	concert	ks/
compliance	kp,	concession	ksj
complicate	kpka	concise	ksı
compliment	kp—	conclave	kkv
complimentary	kp—y	conclude	kku
comply	kpı	conclusion	kkj
component	kpn—	conclusive	kksv
compose	kpz	concrete	kke
composition	kpzj	condemn	kdm
compound	kp—	condense	kd,
comprehend	kph—	condition	kdj
comprehensive	kphnsv	conditioner	kdjr
compress	kps	conditioning	kdjg
compression	kpj	conduct	kdk
compromise	kpmz	conducting	kdkg
comptroller	kllr	confectionery	kfkjy
compute	kpu	confer	kfr
computer	kpur	conference	kfr,
computing	kpug	confess	kfs
comrade	krd	confession	kfj
conceal	kse	confidence	kfd,
conceit	kse	confident	kfd—
conceivable	ksvB	confidential	kfdnx
conceive	ksv	confine	kfı

confinement	kf—	considerable	ksdrB
confining	kfig	consideration	ksdrj
confirm	kfm	considering	ksdrg
confirmation	kfmj	consist	ksS
confirming	kfmg	consistent	ksS—
conflict	kfk	consistently	ksS— l
conflicting	kfkg	consisting	ksSg
confront	kf—	consolidate	kslda
confuse	kfz	consolidation	ksldj
confusion	kfj	conspicuous	kspks
congenial	kgnl	conspiracy	ksprc
congress	kgs	constant	kS—
congressional	kgjl	constantly	kS— l
congressman	kgsmn	constitute	kSlu
connect	knk	constitution	kSlj
connection	knkj	constitutional	kSljl
conquer	kqr	construct	kSk
conscience	kz,	construction	kSkj
conscientious	kznx	constructive	kSkv
conscious	kx	consult	ksl
consciousness	kxns	consultant	ksl—
consecutive	kskv	consultation	kslj
consensus	ksnss	consume	ksu
consent	ks—	consumer	ksur
consequence	ksq,	contact	klk
consequently	ksq— l	contacting	klkg
conservation	ksvj	contain	kla
conservative	ksvv	container	klar
consider	ksdr	containing	klag

contaminate	klmna
contemplate	klmpa
contemplating	klmpag
contemporary	klmpry
contend	kl—
content	kl—
contest	klS
continent	kln—
contingent	klnj—
continue	klnu
continuous	klnus
continuously	klnusl
contract	klk
contracting	klkg
contractor	klkr
contradict	kldk
contrary	kly
contrast	klS
contribute	klbu
contributing	klbug
contribution	klbj
control	klo
controller	klor
controversy	klvc
convalescence	kvls,
convenience	kvn,
convenient	kvn—
conveniently	kvn—l
convention	kvnj
conventional	kvnjl
conversation	kvsj
convert	kv/
convertible	$kv/^{B}$
convey	kva
convict	kvk
conviction	kvkj
convince	kv,
cook	kk
cool	ku
cooperate	kopra
cooperation	koprj
cooperative	koprv
coordinate	ko^{na}
coordinator	ko^{nar}
cope	ko
copper	kpr
copy	kp
cord	k/
cordial	kjl
cordially	kjll
core	ko
cork	k/
corkscrew	k^{sku}
corn	kn
corner	knr
corporate	crp
corporately	crp
corporation	crp

corporative	crp	county	knt
corps	ko	coup	ku
correct	krk	couple	kpl
correcting	krkg	coupon	qpn
correction	krkj	courage	krj
corrective	krkv	course	ks
correctly	krkl	court	k/
correspond	krsp	courteous	k/x
correspondence	krsp,	courtesy	k/c
corresponding	krsp g	cover	kvr
corridor	krdr	coverage	kvrj
corrosion	krj	covering	kvrg
corrugated	krga	cow	kw
cosmetic	kzmtk	crack	kk
cost	kS	craft	kf
costly	kSl	crane	ka
costume	kSu	crash	kz
cottage	ktj	crawl	kl
cotton	ktn	crazy	kz
couch	kwc	creak	ke
could	kd	cream	ke
council	kwnsl	create	ka
counsel	kwnsl	creation	kj
counselor	kwnslr	creative	kav
count	k	creator	kar
counter	k	creature	kcr
counteract	kak	credential	kdnx
counterfeit	kft	credit	kdt
country	k y	crediting	kdtg

crew	ku
crime	ki
criminal	kmnl
crisis	kss
critic	klk
critical	klkl
criticism	klszm
crop	kp
cross	ks
crossroad	ksro
crosstown	kslwn
crosswalk	kswk
crowd	kwd
crucial	kx
crude	ku
cruel	ku
cruelty	kul
cruise	kz
crush	kz
crust	kS
cry	ki
crystal	kSl
cue	q
cuff	kf
cultivate	klva
cultural	kcrl
culture	kcr
cup	kp
curb	kb
cure	ku
curious	krx
currency	krnc
current	kr—
currently	kr—l
curricula	krkla
curriculum	krklm
cursory	ksy
curtail	k^{a}
curve	kv
cushion	kj
custom	kSm
customary	kSmy
customer	kSmr
cut	kl
cutting	klg
cycle	skl

D

daily	Dl
dairy	dy
dam	dm
damage	dmj
damaging	dmjg
damp	dm

dance	d,
dancing	dnsg
danger	dnjr
dangerous	dnjrs
dare	da
dark	d/
darkness	d/ns
dash	dz
data	dla
date	da
dating	dag
daughter	dlr
dawn	dn
day	D
daylight	Dli
daytime	Dli
dead	dd
deadline	ddli
deadly	ddl
deaf	df
deal	de
dealer	der
dealing	deg
dean	de
dear	de
death	d_
debate	dba
debit	dbl
debt	dl
decade	dka
decay	dk
deceased	dse
deceive	dsv
December	Dc
decent	ds_
decide	dsi
deciding	dsig
decision	dsj
deck	dk
declaration	dkrj
declare	dka
decline	dki
decontrol	dklo
decorate	dkra
decoration	dkrj
decrease	dke
dedicate	ddka
dedication	ddkj
deduce	ddu
deduct	ddk
deductible	ddkB
deduction	ddkj
deed	de
deem	de
deep	de
deeply	del
deer	de
defaulting	dflg

defeat	dfe
defect	dfk
defection	dfkj
defective	dfkv
defend	df—
defendant	df——
defense	df,
defer	dfr
defiance	dfi,
deficiency	dfznc
deficient	dfz—
deficit	dfsl
define	dfi
definite	dfnl
definitely	dfnll
definition	dfnj
definitive	dfnv
defrost	dfS
defy	dfi
degree	dge
delay	dla
delaying	dlag
delegate (*n.*)	dlgl
delegate (*vb.*)	dlga
delegation	dlgj
delete	dle
deliberately	dlbrll
deliberation	dlbrj
delicate	dlkl
delicatessen	dlklsn
delicious	dlx
delight	dli
delightful	dlf
delinquent	dlgg—
deliver	dlvr
delivery	dlvy
deluxe	dlx
demand	d—
demanding	d—g
democracy	dmkc
democratic	dmklk
demonstrate	dmnSa
demonstrating	dmnSag
demonstration	dmnSj
demonstrator	dmnSar
deniable	dniB
denomination	dnmnj
denote	dno
dense	d,
dental	d—l
dentist	d—S
dentistry	d—Sy
deny	dni
depart	dp/
department	dp/—
departmental	dp/—l
departure	dpcr
depend	dp—

dependability	dp—bll
dependable	dp—B
dependent	dp—
depending	dp—g
deplete	dpe
deport	dp/
deposit	dpzl
depositary	dpzly
depreciable	dpzB
depreciation	dpzj
depress	dps
depression	dpj
deprive	dpv
depth	dp—
derive	drv
descendant	ds—
descent	ds—
describe	dki
describing	dkig
description	dkpj
descriptive	dkpv
desert	dz/
deserve	dzv
design	dzi
designate	dzgna
designer	dzir
desirable	dziB
desire	dzi
desiring	dzig
desk	ds
despair	dpa
desperate	dprl
desperation	dprj
despise	dpz
despite	dpi
despondent	dp—
despotic	dplk
destination	dSnj
destiny	dSne
destitute	dSlu
destroy	dSy
destruction	dSkj
detach	dlc
detachable	dlcB
detachment	dlc—
detail	dla
detect	dlk
detective	dlkv
determination	dlmnj
determine	dlmn
determining	dlmng
detest	dlS
detour	dlu
develop	dvlp
developing	dvlpg
development	dvlp—
device	dvi
devious	dvx

devise	dvz
devote	dvo
devotion	dvj
devout	dvwl
diagnosis	dgnss
dial	di
diameter	dmtr
diamond	dm—
dictate	dkla
dictation	dklj
dictionary	dkjy
did	d
die	di
diet	dl
differ	dfr
difference	dfr,
different	dfr—
difficult	dfkl
difficulty	dfkl
digest	djS
digestive	djSv
dignify	dgnfi
dignity	dgnl
dilute	dlu
dime	di
dimension	dmnj
diminish	dmnz
dine	di
dining	dig

dinner	dnr
diploma	dpma
direct	drk
direction	drkj
directional	drkjl
directly	drkl
director	drkr
directory	drky
dirt	d/
dirty	d/e
disability	dabll
disable	daB
disagree	dage
disagreeable	dageB
disallow	dalw
disappear	dape
disappoint	dapy—
disappointment	dapy—
disaster	dzSr
disband	db—
discard	dk/
discharge	dcj
discipline	dpn
disclose	dkz
disclosure	dkzr
discomfort	dkf/
discontent	dkl—
discontinue	dklnu
discount	dk—

discourage	dkrj	dissatisfied	dsl
discover	dkvr	dissolve	dzv
discovery	dkvy	distance	dS,
discriminate	dkmna	distant	dS—
discriminating	dkmnag	distill	dSl
discrimination	dkmnj	distinct	dSq
discuss	dks	distinction	dSqj
discussing	dksg	distinctive	dSqv
discussion	dkj	distinguish	dSgwz
disease	dzz	distribute	dSbu
disengage	dngj	distributing	dSbug
disfavor	dfvr	distribution	dSbj
disgrace	dga	distributor	dSbur
dish	dz	district	dSk
disk	ds	distrust	dSS
dislike	dli	disturb	dSb
dismantle	dm—l	disturbance	dSb,
dismay	dma	diversify	dvsfi
dismiss	dms	diversion	dvj
disorder	do^r	divert	dv—
dispatch	dpc	divide	dvi
display	dpa	dividend	dvd—
displaying	dpag	divinity	dvnl
disposable	dpzB	division	dvj
disposal	dpzl	divisional	dvjl
dispose	dpz	divorce	dvs
disposing	dpzg	do	d
disposition	dpzj	dock	dk
dispute	dpu	doctor	dkbr

doctrine	dkln
document	dk—
does	dz
dog	dg
doing	d
dollar	dlr
domestic	dmSk
dominance	dmn,
dominant	dmn—
dominate	dmna
donation	dnj
done	d
doom	du
door	do
dosage	doj
dot	dl
double	dB
doubt	dwl
doughnut	donl
down	dwn
downtown	dwnlwn
downward	dwn/
doze	dz
dozen	dzn
draft	df
drag	dg
drain	da
drama	dma
dramatic	dmlk

drapery	day
drapes	da
draw	da
drawer	do
drawing	dag
drawn	dan
dread	dd
dreadful	ddf
dream	de
dress	ds
dressing	dsg
drew	du
drift	df
drill	dl
drink	dg
drive	dv
drive-in	dvn
driven	dvn
driver	dvr
driveway	dvwa
driving	dvg
drop	dp
dropping	dpg
drove	dv
drown	dwn
drug	dg
druggist	dgS
drum	dm
dry	di

dryer	dir
drying	dig
dual	dl
dubious	dbx
duck	dk
due	d
dues	dz
dug	dg
dull	dl
dummy	dme
dump	dm
dungarees	dgre
duplicate (*adj.*)	dpkl
duplicate (*vb.*)	dpka
duplicating	dpkag
duplication	dpkj
durable	drB
during	drg
dust	dS
duty	dt
dye	di
dynamite	dnmi

E

each	ec
eager	egr
ear	er
earlier	elr
earliest	elS
early	el
earn	en
earnest	enS
earnestly	enSl
earning	eng
earth	e—
earthquake	e—qa
ease	ez
easier	ezr
easily	ezl
east	E
eastern	En
easy	ez
eat	et
eaten	etn
eating	etg
economic	eknmk
economical	eknmkl
economy	eknme
edge	ej
edging	ejg
edition	edj
editor	edtr
editorial	edtrl
educate	ejka

education	ejkj
educational	ejkjl
educator	ejkar
effect	efk
effective	efkv
effectively	efkvl
efficiency	efznc
efficient	efz—
efficiently	efz—l
effort	f
egg	eg
either	e—r
eject	ejk
elderly	ldrl
elect	elk
election	elkj
electric	elklk
electrical	elklkl
electrician	elklj
electricity	elklsl
electronic	elklnk
elegance	lgs
elegant	lg—
element	l—
elementary	l—y
elevate	lva
elevation	lvj
elevator	lvar
eligibility	ljbll
eligible	ljB
eliminate	elmna
eliminating	elmnag
elimination	elmnj
eloquent	lq—
else	ls
elsewhere	lswa
embarrass	mbrs
embezzle	mbzl
emblem	mbm
embrace	mba
emerald	mrd
emerge	emj
emergency	emjnc
emotion	emj
emphasis	mfss
emphasize	mfsz
employ	mpy
employee	mpye
employer	mpyr
employing	mpyg
employment	mpy—
empty	ml
enable	naB
enabling	naBg
enact	nak
enclose	nkz
enclosing	nkzg
enclosure	nkzr

encounter	nk_r	enlist	nlS
encourage	nkrj	enlistment	nlS—
encouragement	nkrj—	enormous	enms
encouraging	nkrjg	enough	enf
encyclopedia	nskpda	enrich	nrc
end	—	enroll	nro
endanger	ndnjr	enrollment	nro—
endeavor	ndvr	ensuing	nsug
ending	—g	enter	N
endorse	nds	entering	Ng
endorsement	nds—	enterprise	Npz
endow	ndw	entertain	Nla
endowment	ndw—	entertaining	Nlag
endurance	ndu,	entertainment	Nla—
endure	ndu	enthusiasm	n–zzm
enemy	nme	entire	nli
energy	ng	entirely	nlil
enforce	nfs	entirety	nlil
enforcement	nfs—	entitle	nlll
engage	ngj	entrance	N,
engagement	ngj—	entry	Ne
engine	njn	envelope	nvlo
engineer	njne	enviable	nvB
engineering	njneg	envious	nvx
enjoy	njy	environment	nvrn—
enjoyable	njyB	envy	nv
enjoying	njyg	equal	eql
enjoyment	njy—	equality	eqll
enlarge	nlj	equally	eqll

equip	eqp
equipment	eqp—
equitable	eqlB
equivalent	eqvl—
erase	era
erect	erk
errand	er—
error	err
erupt	erp
escape	ska
escort	sk/
especially	espxl
essence	s,
essential	esnx
establish	eSbz
establishing	eSbzg
establishment	eSbz—
estate	eSa
esteem	eSe
estimate (*n.*)	eSml
estimate (*vb.*)	eSma
estimating	eSmag
eternal	etnl
evaluate	evla
evaporate	evpra
even	ev
evening	evng
event	ev—
eventually	evncll
ever	ev
every	ev
everybody	evbd
everyday	evD
everyone	evwn
everything	ev—g
everywhere	evwa
evidence	evd,
evident	evd—
evidently	evd—l
evolve	evv
exact	xk
exactly	xkl
examination	xmnj
examine	xmn
examiner	xmnr
examining	xmng
example	xmpl
exceed	xse
exceeding	xseg
excellence	xl,
excellent	xl—
except	xsp
excepting	xspg
exception	xspj
exceptional	xspjl
excess	xss
excessive	xssv
exchange	xcnj

exchangeable	xcnjB	expanding	xp—g
excise	xsz	expanse	xp,
excite	xsi	expansion	xpnj
excitement	xsi—	expect	xpk
exciting	xsig	expecting	xpkg
exclaim	xka	expedite	xpdi
exclude	xku	expedition	xpdj
exclusive	xksv	expenditure	xp—cr
exclusively	xksvl	expense	xp,
excursion	xkj	expensive	xpnsv
excuse (*n.*)	xku	experience	xpr,
excuse (*vb.*)	xkz	experimental	xpr—l
execute	xku	expert	xp/
executive	xkv	expiration	xpry
exempt	xmp	expire	xpi
exemption	xmpj	explain	xpa
exercise	xsz	explaining	xpag
exert	x/	explanation	xpnj
exertion	xj	explanatory	xpnly
exhaust	xS	explore	xpo
exhaustion	xsj	export	xp/
exhaustive	xsv	expose	xpz
exhibit	xbl	exposition	xpzj
exhibition	xbj	express	xps
exist	xS	expressing	xpsg
existence	xS,	expression	xpj
existing	xSg	extend	xl—
exit	xl	extending	xl—g
expand	xp—	extension	xlnj

extensive	xlnsv
extent	xl—
exterior	xlrr
external	xlnl
extinguisher	xlgwzr
extra	xla
extract	xlk
extraordinary	xlo ny
extreme	xle
extremely	xlel
extremist	xleS
eye	i
eyesight	isi
eyewitness	iwlns

F

fabric	fbk
fabricate	fbka
face	fa
facial	fx
facilitate	fslla
facility	fsll
facing	fag
fact	fk
factor	fklr
factory	fkly
factual	fkcl
faculty	fkl
fad	fd
fade	fa
fail	fa
failure	far
faint	f—
fair	fa
fairly	fal
faith	f—
faithful	f7
fake	fa
fall	fl
fallen	fln
false	fs
fame	fa
familiar	fmlr
familiarize	fmlrz
family	fml
famous	fms
fan	fn
fancy	fnc
far	fr
fare	fa
farm	fm
farmer	fmr
farther	fr–r
fascinate	fsna

fashion	fj
fashionable	fjB
fast	fS
fasten	fsn
faster	fSr
fat	fl
fatal	fll
fatality	flll
fate	fa
father	f—r
fatigue	fle
fault	fl
faulty	fl
favor	fvr
favorable	fvrB
favorably	fvrBl
favorite	fvrl
fear	fe
fearful	fef
fearlessly	felsl
feast	fS
feat	fe
feather	f—r
feature	fcr
featuring	fcrg
February	Fb
fed	fd
federal	fdrl
fee	fe
feeble	fB
feed	fe
feeding	feg
feel	fe
feeling	feg
feet	fe
fell	fl
fellow	flo
fellowship	flozp
felony	flne
felt	fl
female	fma
feminine	fmnn
fence	fs
fender	f—r
ferocious	frx
fertilizer	flzr
festival	fSvl
fever	fvr
feverish	fvrz
few	fu
fiber	fbr
fictitious	fklx
fidelity	fdll
field	fd
fierce	fs
fiery	fiy
fifth	ff
fight	fi

fighting	fig	fireworks	fiw
figure	fgr	firm	fm
file	fi	firmly	fml
filing	fig	first	fS
fill	fl	fiscal	fskl
filler	flr	fish	fz
filling	flg	fishing	fzg
film	fm	fit	fl
filter	flr	fitting	flg
final	fnl	five	fv
finalist	fnlS	fix	fx
finality	fnll	fixture	fxcr
finally	fnll	flag	fg
finance	fn,	flagstone	fgSo
financial	fnnx	flame	fa
financing	fnnsg	flap	fp
find	f—	flare	fa
finding	f—g	flash	fz
fine	fi	flashing	fzg
finest	fiS	flashlight	fzli
finger	fgr	flat	fl
finish	fnz	flatter	flr
finishing	fnzg	flavor	fvr
fire	fi	flee	fe
firearm	firm	fleet	fe
fireman	fimn	flesh	fz
fireplace	fipa	flexible	fxB
fireproof	fipu	flight	fi
firewood	fiwd	float	fo

flock	fk
flood	fd
floor	fo
florist	frs
flow	fo
flower	fur
fluid	fd
flush	fz
fly	fi
foam	fo
foe	fo
fog	fg
foil	fyl
fold	fd
folder	fdr
folding	fdg
folk	fo
follow	flo
following	flog
food	fu
fool	fu
foolish	fuz
foot	ft
football	ftbl
for	f
forbid	fbd
force	fs
forecast	fks
foreclosure	fkzr
foreign	frn
foreman	fmn
foremost	fms
foresee	fc
foresight	fsi
forest	frs
forever	fev
forfeit	fft
forgave	fgv
forget	fgt
forgive	fgv
forgiven	fgvn
forgot	fgt
forgotten	fgtn
form	fm
formal	fml
formation	fmj
formative	fmv
former	fmr
formerly	fmrl
formula	fmla
formulate	fmla
fort	f/
forth	f—
forthcoming	f—k
fortify	ffi
fortress	fs
fortunate	fcnt
fortunately	fcntl

forum
forward
forwarding
fought
foul
found
foundation
founder
fountain
fourth
fraction
fragment
frame
framework
franchise
frank
frankly
frantic
fraternal
fraternally
fraud
freak
free
freedom
freeze
freezer
freight
frequency
frequent
frequently
fresh
freshman
Friday
fried
friend
friendly
friendship
fringe
from
front
frontage
frontier
frost
frown
froze
frozen
fruit
frustrate
fry
frying
fudge
fuel
fulfill
fulfillment
full
full-time (*u.m.*)
fullest
fully

fun	fn
function	fgj
fund	f—
fundamental	f—l
funeral	fnrl
funnel	fnl
funny	fne
fur	fr
furious	frx
furnace	fns
furnish	fnz
furnishing	fnzg
furniture	fncr
further	f—r
furthermore	f—rmo
fury	fy
fuse	fz
fuss	fs
futile	ftl
future	fcr

G

gain	ga
gainful	gaf
gallant	gl—
gallery	gly
gallon	gln
gamble	gmB
game	ga
gang	gg
garage	gry
garbage	gby
garden	g^n
garment	g—
gas	gs
gasoline	gsle
gate	ga
gather	g—r
gauge	gj
gauze	gz
gave	gv
gay	ga
gear	ge
gelatin	jltn
gem	jm
general	jnrl
generally	jnrll
generate	jnra
generation	jnrj
generator	jnrar
generosity	jnrsl
generous	jnrs
genius	gns
gentle	j—l

gentleman	j—lmn
genuine	jnn
germ	jm
gesture	jscr
get	gl
getting	glg
ghost	gs
giant	j—
gift	gf
gin	jn
girl	gl
give	gv
given	gvn
giving	gvg
glad	gd
gladly	gdl
glamor	gmr
glance	gs
glare	ga
glass	gs
glassware	gswa
gleam	ge
gleaming	geg
glimpse	gmps
globe	go
glorious	grx
glory	gy
glove	gv
glow	go
glue	gu
go	g
goal	go
goes	g
going	g
gold	gd
golden	gdn
golf	gf
gone	g
good	gd
goodbye	gdb
goodwill	gdl
got	gl
gotten	gln
govern	gvn
governing	gvng
government	gvl
governmental	gvl
governmentalize	gvl
governor	gvnr
gown	gwn
grace	ga
graceful	gaf
gracious	gx
grade	ga
gradual	gjl
gradually	gjll
graduate (*n.*)	gjl
graduate (*vb.*)	gja

graduating	gjag
graduation	gjj
grain	ga
grand	g—
grandfather	g—f—r
grandmother	g—m—r
grant	g—
grape	ga
grass	gs
grate	ga
grateful	gaf
gratifying	glfig
gratitude	gllu
grave	gv
gravity	gvl
gray	ga
grease	ge
great	ga
greater	gar
greatest	gas
greatly	gal
green	ge
greenhouse	gehws
greet	ge
greeting	geg
grew	gu
grief	ge
grievance	gvs
grim	gm
grind	g—
gritty	gl
grocer	gsr
grocery	gsy
groom	gu
grope	go
gross	go
ground	g—
group	gu
grove	gv
grow	go
growing	gog
grown	gon
growth	go—
guarantee	grnl
guaranty	grnl
guard	g/
guardian	gn
guess	gs
guest	gs
guidance	g,
guide	gi
guild	gd
guilty	gl
gulf	gf
gum	gm
gun	gn
guy	gi
gymnasium	jmnzm

H

habit	hbl
habitual	hbcl
had	h
hail	ha
hair	ha
hairdresser	hadsr
half	hf
hall	hl
halt	hl
ham	hm
hamburger	hmbgr
hammer	hmr
hamper	hmpr
hand	h—
handbag	h—bg
handbook	h—bk
handcuff	h—kf
handicap	h—kp
handkerchief	hgkcf
handle	h—l
handling	h—lg
handmade	h—ma
handsome	h—sm
handwriting	h—rig
handy	hnd
hang	hg
hanger	hgr

hanging	hgg
happen	hpn
happiness	hpns
happy	hp
harass	hrs
harbor	hbr
hard	h/
harden	h/n
harder	h/r
hardest	h/$
hardship	h/zp
hardware	h/wa
harm	hm
harmless	hmls
harmony	hmne
harsh	hz
has	hz
hat	hl
hatred	had
haul	hl
haunt	h—
have	h
having	h
hay	ha
hazard	hz/
hazardous	hz/s
he	e

head	hd
headache	hdak
heading	hdg
headlight	hdli
headquarters	hdq^r
heal	he
health	h—
healthy	h—e
hear	he
heard	h/
hearing	heg
heart	h/
heat	he
heater	her
heating	heg
heaven	hvn
heavier	hvr
heavy	hv
hedge	hj
heed	he
heel	he
height	hi
heirloom	arlu
held	hd
helicopter	hlkplr
hello	hlo
help	hp
helpful	hpf
helping	hpg
helpless	hpls
hence	h,
her	r
here	he
hereafter	heaf
herein	hen
hereto	hel
herewith	hew
heritage	hrlj
hero	hro
hers	r
herself	rsf
hesitate	hzla
hesitation	hzlj
hidden	hdn
hide	hi
hideous	hdx
high	hi
higher	hir
highest	his
highlight	hili
highly	hil
highway	hiwa
hike	hi
hill	hl
him	m
himself	msf
hinge	hnj
hint	h—

hire	hi
hiring	hig
his	z
historical	hSrkl
history	hSy
hit	hl
hobby	hb
hold	hd
holding	hdg
hole	ho
holiday	hlD
hollow	hlo
home	ho
homeless	hols
homeowner	hoonr
homicide	hmsi
honest	onS
honestly	onSl
honey	hne
honor	onr
honorable	onrB
honorary	onry
hood	hd
hook	hk
hope	ho
hopeful	hof
hopeless	hols
hoping	hog
horizon	hrzn

horn	hn
horse	hs
horsepower	hspwr
hose	hz
hosiery	hzy
hospital	hspll
hospitality	hsplll
hospitalization	hspllzj
hospitalize	hspllz
host	hS
hostess	hSs
hostile	hSl
hot	hl
hotel	hll
hour	r
hourly	rl
house	hws
housecleaning	hwskeg
household	hwshd
housekeeping	hwskeg
houseware	hwswa
housing	hwzg
how	hw
however	hwev
huge	hj
human	hmn
humane	hma
humidity	hmdl
humor	hmr

hung	hg	hurricane	hrka
hungry	hgy	hurry	hy
hunt	h—	hurt	h/
hunting	h—g	husband	hzb—
hurl	hl	hypothetical	hp—tkl

I

I	I	illustration	ilSj
ice	is	illustrative	ilSv
icy	ic	image	mj
idea	ida	imagination	mjnj
ideal	ide	imagine	mjn
identical	id—kl	imitation	mtj
identifiable	id—fiB	immaterial	imtrl
identification	id—fkj	immediacy	imd
identify	id—fi	immediate	imd
identity	id—t	immediately	imd
idle	idl	immerse	ims
if	f	immigrant	img—
ignition	ignj	immigration	imgj
ignorance	ignr,	immobile	imB
ignorant	ignr—	immobilize	imBz
ignore	igno	immoderate	imdrt
ill	il	immoral	imrl
illness	ilns	immortal	im^{l}
illuminate	ilmna	immune	imu
illusion	ilj	impact	mpk
illustrate	ilSa	impartial	mpx

impassive	mpsv
impede	mpe
impel	mpl
imperative	mprv
imperfect	mpfk
imply	mpi
import	mp/
importance	mp^
important	mp‾
impose	mpz
impossible	mpsB
impress	mps
impression	mpj
impressive	mpsv
imprint	mp—
imprison	mpzn
improper	mppr
improve	mpv
improvement	mpv—
improving	mpvg
impulse	mps
impulsive	mpsv
in	n
inability	nabll
inactivity	nakvl
inadequate	naql
inasmuch	nzmc
inaugurate	nagra
inauguration	nagrj
incapable	nkpB
incentive	ns—v
inch	nc
incident	nsd—
incidentally	nsd—ll
incline	nki
include	nku
including	nkug
inclusive	nksv
income	nk
inconsiderate	nksdrl
inconvenience	nkvn,
incorporate	ncrp
incorporation	ncrp
incorrect	nkrk
increase	nke
increasing	nkeg
increasingly	nkegl
incredible	nkdB
incur	nkr
incurable	nkuB
indebtedness	ndlns
indeed	nde
indefinite	ndfnl
indefinitely	ndfnll
indemnity	ndmnl
independence	ndp,
independent	ndp—
index	ndx

indicate	ndka	inflation	nfj
indicating	ndkag	inflationary	nfjy
indication	ndkj	inflict	nfk
indicative	ndkv	influence	nf,
indictment	nd—	influential	nfnx
indifferent	ndfr—	inform	nfm
indirectly	ndrkl	informal	nfml
indispensable	ndpnsB	informant	nfm—
individual	ndv	information	nfo
individualistic	ndv	informational	nfo
individuality	ndv	informative	nfmv
individualize	ndv	informer	nfmr
individually	ndv	informing	nfmg
indoor	ndo	ingenuity	njnl
industrial	ndSl	ingredient	ngd—
industry	ndSy	inhabit	nhbl
inefficiency	nefznc	inherit	nhrl
inevitable	nevlB	initial	nx
inexpensive	nxpnsv	initiation	nzj
inexperience	nxpr,	initiative	nzv
infancy	nfnc	injection	njkj
infant	nf—	injure	njr
infect	nfk	injury	njy
inferior	nfrr	ink	ig
infest	nfS	inland	nl—
infiltrate	nfla	inmate	nma
infirmary	nfmy	inn	n
inflammable	nfmB	inner	nr
inflate	nfa	innocence	ns,

innocent	ns—
innovation	nvj
inoculation	nklj
input	npl
inquire	nqi
inquiring	nqig
inquiry	nqiy
inquisitive	nqzv
insane	nsa
insanity	nsnl
insect	nsk
insert	ns/
inserting	ns/g
insertion	nsj
inside	nsi
insist	nsS
insistence	nsS,
insofar	nofr
inspect	nspk
inspection	nspkj
inspector	nspkr
inspiration	nspry
inspire	nspi
install	nSl
installation	nSlj
installment	nSl—
instance	nS,
instant	nS—
instantly	nS—l
instead	nSd
instinct	nSg
institute	nSlu
institution	nSlj
institutional	nSljl
instruct	nSk
instruction	nSkj
instructor	nSkr
instrument	nS—
instrumental	nS—l
insulate	nsla
insulation	nslj
insult	nsl
insurance	nzu,
insure	nzu
intact	nlk
integral	nlgl
integrity	nlgl
intelligence	nllj,
intelligent	nllj—
intend	nl—
intensity	nlnsl
intensive	nlnsv
intent	nl—
intention	nlnj
interchange	Ncnj
interest	NS
interesting	NSg
interfere	Nfe

interim	Nm	invade	nva
interior	Nr	invalid	nvld
interject	Njk	invasion	nvj
intermediate	Nmdl	invent	nv—
intermit	Nml	invention	nvnj
intermix	Nmx	inventory	nv—y
internal	Nnl	invest	nvS
international	Nnjl	investigate	nvSga
interpret	Npl	investigating	nvSgag
interpretation	Nplj	investigation	nvSgj
interracial	Nrx	investigator	nvSgar
interrupt	Nrp	investment	nvS—
interruption	Nrpj	investor	nvSr
intersect	Nsk	invisible	nvzB
intersection	Nskj	invitation	nvlj
interstate	NSa	invite	nvi
interval	Nvl	invoice	nvys
intervene	Nve	involve	nvv
interview	Nvu	inward	n/
interviewer	Nvur	iron	irn
interworking	Nw—g	irregular	irglr
intimate (*adj.*)	nlml	irritable	irlB
intimate (*vb.*)	nlma	irritate	irla
into	nl	irritating	irlag
intrastate	NaSa	is	i
introduce	Ndu	island	il—
introducing	Ndug	issue	izu
introduction	Ndkj	issuing	izug
introductory	Ndkly	it	i

item	ilm	itself	isf
itemize	ilmz	ivory	ivy
its	i	ivy	iv

J

jacket	jkl	judge	jj
jail	ja	judging	jjg
janitor	jnlr	judgment	jj—
January	Ja	judicial	jdx
jealous	jls	judiciary	jdzy
jeopardy	jpd	judicious	jdx
jet	jl	jug	jg
jewel	ju	juice	ju
jeweler	jur	July	Jl
jewelry	juy	jump	jm
job	jb	junction	jgj
jobber	jbr	June	Ju
join	jyn	junior	jnr
joining	jyng	junk	jg
joint	jy—	jurisdiction	jrsdkj
jointly	jy—l	juror	jrr
jot	jl	jury	jy
journal	jnl	just	jS
journalism	jnlzm	justice	jSs
journalist	jnlS	justifiable	jSfiB
journey	jne	justification	jSfkj
joy	jy	justify	jSfi
joyful	jy¬	juvenile	jvnl

K

keen	ke	kindly	k—l
keep	ke	kindness	k—ns
keeping	keg	king	kg
kennel	knl	kiss	ks
kept	kp	kit	kt
key	ke	kitchen	kcn
keyboard	keb/	knack	nk
kick	kk	knee	ne
kid	kd	knew	nu
kill	kl	knife	ni
killer	klr	knit	nt
killing	klg	know	n
kilowatt	klwt	knowing	ng
kind	k—	knowledge	nlj
kindest	k—s	known	nn

L

label	lB	lake	la
labor	lbr	lame	la
laboratory	lbrly	laminate	lmna
laborer	lbrr	lamp	lm
lack	lk	land	l—
lacquer	lkr	landing	l—g
lading	lag	landlord	l—l
lady	ld	landscape	l—ska
laid	la	lane	la

language	lgwj
lantern	l—n
lapse	lps
large	lj
largely	ljl
largest	ljS
lash	lz
last	lS
lasting	lSg
late	la
lately	lal
later	lar
latest	laS
latter	ltr
laugh	lf
laughter	lftr
launch	lnc
launder	l—r
laundry	l—y
lavender	lv—r
law	la
lawful	laf
lawn	ln
lawyer	lyr
lay	la
layoff	laof
layout	lao
lead (*n.*)	ld
lead (*vb.*)	le
leader	ler
leadership	lerzp
leading	leg
leaf	le
leaflet	lelt
league	le
leak	le
lean	le
leap	le
learn	ln
learning	lng
lease	le
leash	lz
least	lS
leather	l—r
leave	lv
leaving	lvg
lecture	lkcr
led	ld
ledger	ljr
left	lf
leg	lg
legal	lgl
legible	ljB
legibly	ljBl
legislation	ljsj
legislative	ljsv
legislature	ljscr
leisure	lzr

lend
lender
length
lens
less
lesser
lesson
let
letter
letterhead
letting
level
lever
levy
liability
liable
libel
liberal
liberty
librarian
library
license
lie
lien
lieu
lieutenant
life
lifetime
lift
light
lighting
lightning
like
likely
likewise
limb
limit
limitation
limousine
line
linen
linger
lining
link
liquid
liquidation
list
listen
listing
lit
literally
literature
little
live
livelihood
liver
livestock
living

load	lo	lose	lz
loading	log	losing	lzg
loaf	lo	loss	ls
loan	lo	lost	ls
lobster	lbsr	lot	ll
local	lkl	lotion	lj
locality	lkll	loud	lwd
locally	lkll	loudly	lwdl
locate	lka	lounge	lwnj
locating	lkag	love	lv
location	lkj	lovely	lvl
lock	lk	low	lo
locksmith	lksm—	lower	lor
locomotive	lkmv	lowest	los
lodge	lj	loyal	lyl
lodging	ljg	loyalty	lyll
loft	lf	lubricate	lbka
logical	ljkl	lubrication	lbkj
lone	lo	luck	lk
lonely	lol	luckily	lkl
lonesome	losm	lucrative	lkv
long	lg	luggage	lgj
longer	lgr	lumber	lmbr
longing	lgg	lunch	lnc
look	lk	luncheon	lncn
looking	lkg	lure	lu
loop	lu	luxurious	lxrx
loose	lu	luxury	lxy
loot	lu	lying	lig

M

machine	mze	manage	mnj
machinery	mzey	management	mnj—
machinist	mzeS	manager	mnjr
mad	md	managerial	mnjrl
madam	mdm	managing	mnjg
made	ma	maneuver	mnvr
magazine	mgze	manila	mnla
magic	mjk	mankind	mnk—
magical	mjkl	manner	mnr
magnificent	mgnfs—	mansion	mnj
magnify	mgnfi	manual	mnl
mahogany	mhgne	manufacture	mf
maid	ma	manufacturer	mf
mail	ma	manufacturing	mf
mailing	mag	manuscript	mnskp
main	ma	many	m
maintain	m—a	map	mp
maintaining	m—ag	maple	mpl
maintenance	m—n,	marble	mB
major	mjr	March	Mr
majority	mjrl	margarine	mjrn
make	ma	margin	mjn
maker	mar	marine	mre
making	mag	martial	mx
male	ma	mark	m/
malicious	mlx	market	m/t
man	mn	marketing	m/g

marking	m/g
marriage	mrj
marry	my
marshal	mx
marvel	mvl
marvelous	mvls
mask	ms
mass	ms
massage	msj
massive	msv
mast	ms
master	msr
masterfully	msrf
mat	mt
match	mc
material	mtrl
materially	mtrll
maternity	mtnt
mathematics	m—mtx
matter	mtr
mattress	mts
mature	mcu
maturity	mcut
maximum	mxmm
may	ma
May	Ma
maybe	mab
mayor	mr
maze	mz
me	e
meal	me
mean	me
meaning	meg
meant	m—
meantime	met
meanwhile	mewi
measure	mzr
meat	me
mechanic	mknk
mechanical	mknkl
medal	mdl
mediation	mdj
medical	mdkl
medicine	mdsn
medium	mdm
meet	me
meeting	meg
melt	mt
member	mmbr
membership	mmbrzp
memo	mmo
memorandum	mmr—m
memorial	mmrl
memory	mmy
men	mn
menace	mns
mend	m—
mental	m—l

mention	mnj
menu	mnu
merchandise	mds
merchandiser	mds
merchandising	mds
merchant	mc—
mercy	mc
merely	mel
merge	mj
merit	mrl
mesh	mz
mess	ms
message	msj
messenger	msnjr
met	ml
metal	mll
meter	mlr
method	m—d
metropolitan	mlplln
microphone	mkfo
middle	mdl
midnight	mdni
might	mi
mild	md
mile	mi
mileage	mij
military	mlly
milk	mk
mill	ml
millinery	mlny
million	mln
mimeograph	mmgf
mind	m—
mine	m
mineral	mnrl
miniature	mncr
minimum	mnmm
mining	mig
minister	mnSr
mink	mg
minor	mnr
minority	mnrl
minus	mns
minute (*adj.*)	mnu
minute (*n.*)	mnl
miracle	mrkl
miraculous	mrkls
mirror	mrr
misapply	mapi
misbecoming	mbk
misbehave	mbhv
misbehaving	mbhvg
misbrand	mb—
miscellaneous	mlnx
mischief	mcf
miscount	mk—
misdemeanor	mdmnr
misdirect	mdrk

miserable	mzrB
misery	mzy
misfit	mft
misfortune	mfcn
misgiving	mgvg
mishandle	mh—l
mishandling	mh—lg
mishap	mhp
misjudge	mjj
mislay	mla
mismatch	mmc
misplace	mpa
misprint	mp—
misrepresentation	mrp
miss	ms
missile	msl
missing	msg
mission	mj
misspell	mspl
misspend	msp—
mist	mS
mistake	mSa
mistaken	mSan
mistrust	mSS
misunderstanding	mUSg
misuse (*n.*)	mus
misuse (*vb.*)	muz
mix	mx
mixture	mxcr
mob	mb
mobile	mB
mobilization	mBzj
model	mdl
moderate (*adj.*)	mdrt
moderate (*vb.*)	mdra
modern	mdn
modest	mdS
modifiable	mdfB
moist	myS
moisture	myscr
mold	md
moment	m—
Monday	Mn
money	mne
monitor	mntr
monopoly	mnpl
month	M
monthly	Ml
monument	mn—
moon	mu
moral	mrl
morale	mrl
more	mo
morning	mng
mortal	mtl
mortgage	mgj
mortgagee	mgje
mortgagor	mgjr

most	mS
mostly	mSl
motel	mll
mother	m_r
motion	mj
motor	mlr
motorcycle	mlrskl
motto	mlo
mount	m—
mountain	m—n
mounting	m—g
mouth	mw—
move	mv
movement	mv—
movie	mv
moving	mvg
mow	mo
mower	mor
much	mc
muffler	mfr
multiple	mlpl
multiply	mlpi
municipal	mnspl
museum	mzm
music	mzk
musical	mzkl
must	mS
mutual	mcl
my	m
myself	msf
mysterious	mSrx
mystery	mSy

N

nail	na
name	na
namely	nal
napkin	npkn
narcotic	nklk
narrow	nro
nation	nj
national	njl
nationality	njll
nationally	njll
nationwide	njwi
native	nv
natural	ncrl
naturally	ncrll
nature	ncr
nautical	nlkl
navy	nv
near	ne
nearby	neb
nearest	neS

nearly	nel
neat	ne
necessary	nssy
necessity	nssl
neck	nk
need	ne
needful	nef
needing	neg
needle	ndl
needless	nels
needlessly	nelsl
negative	ngv
neglect	ngk
neglectfully	ngkf
negligence	ngj,
neighbor	nbr
neighborhood	nbrhd
neighboring	nbrg
neither	n
neon	nn
nerve	nv
nervous	nvs
nest	nS
net	nl
network	nlw
never	nv
new	nu
newly	nul
news	nz

newsletter	nzllr
newsmen	nzmn
newspaper	nzppr
next	nx
nice	ni
nicely	nil
nickel	nkl
niece	ne
night	ni
no	n
noble	nB
nobody	nbd
noise	nyz
noiseless	nyzls
nominal	nmnl
nominate	nmna
nominating	nmnag
nominee	nmne
none	n
nonprofit	npfl
nonsense	ns,
nonstop	nSp
noon	nu
nor	n
normal	nml
normally	nmll
north	N
northern	Nn
northwest	NW

nose	nz	novel	nvl
not	n	novelist	nvlS
notable	noB	November	Nv
notably	noBl	now	nw
notary	nty	nucleus	nkx
notation	noj	number	nmbr
note	no	numbering	nmbrg
nothing	n—g	numeral	nmrl
notice	nts	numerous	nmrs
notification	ntfkj	nurse	ns
notify	ntfi	nursery	nsy
notion	nj	nursing	nsg
notorious	ntrx	nut	nt
nourish	nrz	nutritious	ntx
nourishment	nrz—	nylon	nln

O

oak	ok	obscure	obsku
oar	or	observance	obzv,
oat	ot	observation	obzvj
oath	o—	observe	obzv
obedience	obd,	obsolete	obsle
obey	oba	obstruct	obSk
object	objk	obstruction	obSkj
objection	objkj	obtain	obta
objective	objkv	obtaining	obtag
obligation	obgj	obvious	obvx
oblige	obj	obviously	obvxl

occasion	okj	ointment	y—
occasional	okjl	old	od
occasionally	okjll	older	odr
occupancy	okpnc	oldest	odS
occupant	okp—	olympic	olmpk
occupation	okpj	omit	oml
occupational	okpjl	on	o
occupy	okpi	once	ws
occur	okr	oncoming	ok
occurrence	okrs	one	wn
ocean	oj	only	onl
o'clock	okk	onto	ol
October	Oc	open	opn
odd	od	opening	opng
odor	odr	opera	opra
odorless	odrls	operate	opra
of	v	operating	oprag
off	of	operation	oprj
offend	of—	operator	oprar
offense	ofs	opinion	opnn
offensive	ofnsv	opponent	opn—
offer	ofr	opportune	op
offering	ofrg	opportunely	op
office	ofs	opportunism	op
officer	ofsr	opportunist	op
official	ofx	opportunity	op
officially	ofxl	oppose	opz
often	of	opposing	opzg
oil	yl	opposite	opzl

opposition	obzz
oppress	ops
optical	oplkl
optician	oplj
optimistic	oplmsk
option	opj
optional	opjl
or	o
oral	orl
orange	ornj
orbit	obl
orchard	oc/
orchestra	oksa
ordeal	o^e
order	o^r
ordering	o^rg
ordinance	o^n,
ordinarily	o^nrl
ordinary	o^ny
ore	or
organic	ognk
organizable	og
organization	og
organizational	og
organize	og
organizer	og
organizing	og
oriental	or—l
orientation	or—j

origin	orjn
original	orjnl
originally	orjnll
originating	orjnag
ornamental	on—l
orphan	ofn
other	o—r
otherwise	o—ryz
ought	ol
ounce	ow,
our	r
ours	r
ourselves	rsvz
out	O
outboard	Ob
outcome	Ok
outdoor	Odo
outlet	Oll
outline	Oli
outlining	Olig
outlook	Olk
outlying	Olig
output	Opl
outrage	Ory
outside	Osi
outstanding	Osg
outward	O/
oven	ovn
over	V

overage	Vaj
overall	Vl
overcome	Vk
overhead	Vhd
overnight	Vni
overtake	Vta
overtime	Vti
overturn	Vtn
overwhelming	Vwmg
owe	o
own	on
owner	onr
ownership	onrzp
oxygen	oxjn

P

p.m.	p
pace	pa
pack	pk
package	pkj
packaging	pkjg
packets	pkt
packing	pkg
pad	pd
page	pj
paid	pa̲
paid-up	pa̲p
pail	pa
pain	pa
paint	p—
painting	p—g
pair	pa
palace	pls
pale	pa
palm	pm
pamphlet	pmfl
pan	pn
panel	pnl
paneling	pnlg
paper	ppr
parade	pra
paragraph	prgf
parallel	prll
paralysis	prlss
parasite	prsi
parcel	psl
pardon	p⁀n
pardonable	p⁀nB
parent	pr—
parity	prt
park	p⁀
parking	p⁀g
parkway	p⁀wa
parole	pro

part	p/
partial	px
participate	p spa
participating	p spag
participation	p spj
particular	prl
particularity	prl
particularly	prl
partition	pt
partner	p nr
part-time	p ti
party	p e
pass	ps
passage	psj
passenger	psnjr
passing	psg
past	pS
paste	pS
pastor	pSr
pastry	pSy
pasture	pscr
patch	pc
patent	pl—
path	p—
patience	pzs
patient	pz—
patio	plo
patriotic	pllk
patrolman	plomn
patron	pln
pattern	pln
pause	pz
pave	pv
pavement	pv—
pavilion	pvln
pawn	pn
pay	pa
payable	paB
payee	pae
paying	pag
payment	pa—
payroll	paro
peace	pe
peaceable	peB
peacetime	peti
peak	pe
pear	pa
pearl	pl
pecan	pkn
peculiar	pklr
pedal	pdl
pedestrian	pdSn
peel	pe
peer	pe
pen	pn
penalty	pnl
pencil	pnsl
pendant	p—

pending	p—g
penetrate	pnta
pennant	pn—
penny	pne
pension	pnj
people	ppl
pep	pp
pepper	ppr
per	pr
percent	ps—
percentage	ps—j
perfect	pfk
perfection	pfkj
perfectly	pfkl
perform	pfm
performance	pfm,
perfume	pfu
perhaps	php
period	prd
perjury	pjy
permanent	pmn—
permissible	pmsB
permission	pmj
permit	pml
perpetuate	ppca
persecute	psku
persist	psS
persistent	psS—
person	psn
personal	psnl
personality	psnll
personalized	psnlz-
personally	psnll
personnel	psnl
persuade	pswa
pertain	p^{a}
pertaining	p^{ag}
pertinent	p^{n}—
pet	pl
petition	plj
petroleum	pllm
pharmacy	fmc
phase	fz
philosophy	flsfe
phone	fo
phosphate	fsfa
phosphorous	fsfrs
photo	flo
photograph	flgf
photostat	flSl
phrase	fz
physical	fzkl
physician	fzj
piano	pno
pick	pk
picket	pkl
picking	pkg
pickup	pkp

picnic	pknk
picture	pkcr
pie	pi
piece	pe
pier	pe
pile	pi
pill	pl
pillow	plo
pilot	pll
pin	pn
pine	pi
pink	pq
pioneer	pne
pipe	pi
pistol	pSl
piston	pSn
pitch	pc
pity	pl
placard	pk/
place	pa
placement	pa—
plain	pa
plan	pn
plane	pa
planet	pnl
plank	pq
planning	png
plant	p—
plaster	pSr
plastic	pSk
plate	pa
platform	plfm
play	pa
playground	pag—
playing	pag
plea	pe
pleasant	pz—
please	pz
pleasing	pzg
pleasure	pzr
pledge	pj
pledging	pjg
plentiful	p—7
plentifully	p—7
plenty	pnl
plot	pl
plow	pw
plumber	pmr
plumbing	pmg
plunge	pnj
plus	ps
plywood	piwd
pocket	pkl
pocketbook	pklbk
point	py—
poison	pyzn
poisonous	pyzns
pole	po

police	ple
policy	plc
policyholder	plchdr
polio	plo
polish	plz
polite	plr
political	pllkl
politician	plly
politics	pllx
pollute	plu
pollution	ply
pool	pu
poor	pu
pop	pp
poppy	pp
popular	pplr
popularity	pplrl
population	pply
porch	pc
porous	prs
port	p/
portable	p/B
porter	p/r
portfolio	p/flo
portion	pj
portrait	p/t
position	pzj
positive	pzv
possess	pzs
possession	pzj
possibility	psBll
possible	psB
possibly	psBl
post	pS
postage	pSj
postal	pSl
postcard	pSk
poster	pSr
posting	pSg
postmaster	pSmSr
postpone	pSpo
posture	pscr
pot	pl
potential	plnx
poultry	ply
pound	p—
pour	po
poverty	pv
powder	pwdr
power	pwr
powerful	pwf
practicable	pklkB
practical	pklkl
practically	pklkll
practice	pkls
praise	pz
prank	pg
pray	pa

preach	pc
precaution	pkj
precedence	psd,
preceding	pseg
precinct	psq
precious	px
precise	psi
precision	psj
predicament	pdk—
predict	pdk
prediction	pdkj
prefabricate	pfbka
preface	pfs
prefer	pfr
preference	pfr,
pregnancy	pgnnc
prejudice	pjds
preliminary	plmny
premier	pme
premise	pms
premium	pmm
preparation	ppry
preparatory	pprly
prepare	ppa
preparing	ppag
prepayment	ppa—
prerogative	prgv
prescribe	pski
prescription	pskpj
presence	pz,
present	pz—
presentation	pz—j
presently	pz—l
preserve	pzv
preserving	pzvg
president	pzd—
presidential	pzdnx
press	ps
pressure	pzr
prestige	pSj
presumably	pzuBl
presume	pzu
pretend	pl—
pretentious	plnx
pretty	pl
prevail	pva
prevent	pv—
prevention	pvnj
preview	pvu
previous	pvx
previously	pvxl
price	pi
priceless	pils
pricer	pir
pricing	pig
pride	pi
primarily	pmrl
primary	pmy

prime	pi
primitive	pmv
principal	pnspl
principle	pnspl
print	p—
printer	p—r
printing	p—g
prior	pr
priority	prl
privacy	pvc
private	pvl
privilege	pvlj
prize	pz
probability	pbbll
probable	pbB
probably	pbBl
probation	pbj
probe	po
problem	pbm
procedure	psjr
proceed	pse
proceeding	pseg
process	pss
processing	pssg
procession	psj
procure	pku
procurement	pku—
produce	pdu
producer	pdur
producing	pdug
product	pdk
production	pdkj
productive	pdkv
productivity	pdkvl
profession	pfj
professional	pfjl
professor	pfsr
profit	pfl
profitable	pflB
program	pgm
programmer	pgmr
progress	pgs
progressive	pgsv
prohibit	phbl
project	pjk
projector	pjkr
prolong	plg
prominent	pmn—
promise	pms
promising	pmsg
promote	pmo
promoting	pmog
promotion	pmj
promotional	pmjl
prompt	pmp
promptly	pmpl
pronounce	pnws
pronouncement	pnwns—

proof	pu
propaganda	ppg—a
propel	ppl
propeller	pplr
proper	ppr
properly	pprl
property	pp
proportion	ppj
proportionally	ppjll
proposal	ppzl
propose	ppz
proposition	ppzj
prorate	pra
prosecute	psku
prosecution	pskj
prospect	pspk
prospective	pspkv
prospectus	pspkls
prosperity	psprl
prosperous	psprs
protect	plk
protecting	plkg
protection	plkj
protective	plkv
protest	pls
Protestant	pls—
proud	pwd
prove	pv
proven	pvn
provide	pvi
providing	pvig
proving	pvg
provision	pvj
provoke	pvo
proxy	pxe
prudent	pd—
psychologist	skljs
public	pbk
publication	pbkj
publicity	pbsl
publicize	pbsz
publish	pbz
publisher	pbzr
publishing	pbzg
pull	pl
Pullman	plmn
pulse	ps
pump	pm
punch	pnc
punching	pncg
punish	pnz
pupil	ppl
purchase	pcs
purchaser	pcsr
purchasing	pcsg
pure	pu
purpose	pps
purse	ps

pursue	psu	put	pl
pursuit	psu	putting	plg
push	pz	puzzle	pzl

Q

qualification	qlfkj	quicker	qkr
qualify	qlfi	quickly	qkl
quality	qll	quiet	ql
quantity	q—l	quilt	ql
quarrel	qrl	quit	ql
quarry	qy	quite	qi
quart	q/	quiver	qvr
quarter	q/r	quiz	qz
quarterly	q/rl	quorum	qrm
queen	qe	quota	qla
question	qsj	quotation	qoj
questionnaire	qsjna	quote	qo
quick	qk	quoting	qog

R

race	ra	radish	rdz
racial	rx	rag	rg
rack	rk	rage	rj
radar	rdr	raid	ra
radiation	rdj	rail	ra
radiator	rdlr	railroad	raro
radio	rdo	railway	rawa

rain	ra
raincoat	rako
raise	rz
ran	rn
ranch	rnc
random	r—m
rang	rg
range	rnj
ranger	rnjr
ranging	rnjg
rank	rg
ransom	rnsm
rap	rp
rapid	rpd
rapidly	rpdl
rare	ra
rate	ra
rather	r—r
rating	rag
ratio	rzo
rationing	rjg
rave	rv
raw	ra
rayon	rn
reach	rc
reaching	rcg
reaction	rakj
read (*vb.*) (present)	re
read (*vb.*) (past)	rd
readily	rdl
reading	reg
readjustment	rajS—
ready	rd
real	re
realistic	rlSk
realize	rlz
realizing	rlzg
really	rel
realtor	relr
realty	rel
ream	re
rear	re
rearview	revu
reason	rzn
reasonable	rznB
reasonably	rznBl
rebel (*n.*)	rB
rebel (*vb.*)	rbl
rebuilt	rbl
recall	rkl
receipt	rse
receivable	rsvB
receive	rsv
receiver	rsvr
receiving	rsvg
recent	rs—
recently	rs—l
reception	rspj

recess	rss
recipe	rsp
recipient	rsp—
reckless	rkls
recognition	rkgnj
recognize	rkgnz
recommend	rk—
recommendation	rk—j
recommending	rk—g
recondition	rk—j
reconsider	rksdr
record	rk/
recorder	rk/r
recording	rk/g
recount	rk—
recover	rkvr
recovery	rkvy
recreation	rkj
recreational	rkjl
recuperate	rkpra
recurrence	rkr,
red	rd
redeem	rde
redemption	rdmj
reduce	rdu
reducing	rdug
reduction	rdkj
redundant	rd—
reel	re

refer	rfr
reference	rfr,
referendum	rfr—m
referral	rfrl
referring	rfrg
refill	rfl
refine	rfi
refinement	rfi—
refinery	rfiy
refinish	rfnz
reflect	rfk
reform	rfm
refresh	rfz
refreshing	rfzg
refreshment	rfz—
refrigerate	rfjra
refrigeration	rfjrj
refrigerator	rfjrar
refund	rf—
refusal	rfzl
refuse (*n.*)	rfu
refuse (*vb.*)	rfz
regain	rga
regard	rg/
regarding	rg/g
regardless	rg/ls
regency	rjnc
regiment	rj—
region	rjn

regional	rjnl	reliance	rli,
register	rjSr	reliant	rli—
registrant	rjS—	relief	rle
registrar	rjSr	relieve	rlv
registration	rjSj	religion	rljn
registry	rjSy	religious	rljs
regret	rgl	relinquish	rlgqz
regretting	rglg	reluctance	rlkl,
regular	rglr	reluctant	rlkl—
regularly	rglrl	rely	rli
regulate	rgla	remain	rma
regulation	rglj	remainder	rmadr
rehabilitate	rhblla	remaining	rmag
rehabilitation	rhbllj	remark	rm/
reimburse	rmbs	remarkable	rm/B
reinforce	rnfs	remarking	rm/g
reinstate	rnSa	remedial	rmdl
reject	rjk	remedy	rmd
relate	rla	remember	rmmbr
relating	rlag	remind	rm—
relation	rlj	reminder	rm—r
relationship	rljzp	remit	rml
relative	rlv	remittance	rml,
relatively	rlvl	remodel	rmdl
relax	rlx	remote	rmo
relaxation	rlxj	removal	rmvl
relay	rla	remove	rmv
release	rle	removing	rmvg
reliable	rliB	render	r—r

renew	rnu
renewable	rnuB
renewal	rnul
renown	rnwn
rent	r—
rental	r—l
reopen	ropn
reorder	ror
reorganization	rog
reorganize	rog
repaid	rpa
repair	rpa
repairman	rpamn
repay	rpa
repayment	rpa—
repeat	rpe
repetitious	rplx
replace	rpa
replacement	rpa—
replacing	rpag
reply	rpi
replying	rpig
report	rp/
reporting	rp/g
repossess	rpzs
represent	rp
representation	rp
representative	rp
representing	rp

reprint	rp—
reproduce	rpdu
reproduction	rpdkj
republic	rpbk
reputable	rplB
reputation	rplj
request	rqs
requesting	rqsg
require	rqi
requirement	rqi—
requiring	rqig
requisition	rqzj
resale	rsa
rescue	rsq
research	rsc
resent	rz—
reservation	rzvj
reserve	rzv
reservoir	rzvr
residence	rzd,
resident	rzd—
residential	rzdnx
resign	rzi
resignation	rzgnj
resist	rzs
resistance	rzs,
resistant	rzs—
resolution	rzlj
resolve	rzv

resort	rz/
resource	rss
respect	rspk
respectable	rspkB
respectfully	rspkf
respective	rspkv
respectively	rspkvl
respond	rsp—
response	rsps
responsibility	rsp
responsible	rsp
responsive	rspnsv
rest	rS
restaurant	rSr—
restore	rSo
restrain	rSa
restraint	rS—
restrict	rSk
restriction	rSkj
result	rzl
resulting	rzlg
resume	rzu
retail	rla
retailer	rlar
retain	rla
retire	rli
retirement	rli—
return	rln
returnable	rlnB
returning	rlng
reunion	runn
reveal	rve
revenge	rvnj
revenue	rvnu
reverse	rvs
revert	rv/
review	rvu
reviewing	rvug
revise	rvz
revision	rvj
revoke	rvo
revolt	rvl
revolution	rvlj
revolutionary	rvljy
revolve	rvv
revolving	rvvg
reward	r/
rewarding	r/g
rhythm	r—m
rib	rb
ribbon	rbn
rich	rc
rid	rd
ride	ri
rider	rir
ridicule	rdku
ridiculous	rdkls
riding	rig

rigid	ryd
right	ri
right-hand	rih—
rigorous	rgrs
ring	rg
ringing	rgg
rinse	r,
riot	rl
rise	rz
rising	rzg
risk	rs
rival	rvl
river	rvr
road	ro
roadway	rowa
roar	ro
roast	rS
robbery	rby
robe	ro
rock	rk
rocket	rkl
rod	rd
role	ro
roll	ro
roller	ror
rolling	rog
romance	rm,
romantic	rm—k
roof	ru
roofing	rug
room	ru
root	ru
rope	ro
rose	rz
roster	rSr
rotary	rly
rotate	rla
rough	rf
round	r—
round-trip	r—lp
route	ru
routine	rle
routing	rug
row	ro
royal	ryl
rubber	rbr
rubbish	rbz
rude	ru
rug	rg
ruin	rn
rule	ru
rumor	rmr
run	rn
runaway	rnawa
running	rng
rural	rrl
rush	rz
rust	rS

S

sack	sk
sacrifice	skfi
sad	sd
saddle	sdl
sadly	sdl
safe	sa
safeguard	sag/
safety	sal
said	sd
sail	sa
sailing	sag
sailor	sar
saint	s—
sake	sa
salary	sly
sale	sa
salesgirl	sagl
salesman	samn
salon	sln
salt	sl
salvage	svj
same	sa
sample	smpl
sand	s—
sandpaper	s—ppr
sandwich	s—wc
sane	sa
sanitarium	snlrm
sanitary	snly
sanitation	snlj
sank	sg
sarcasm	skzm
sat	sl
satisfaction	sl
satisfactorily	sl
satisfactory	sl
satisfy	sl
satisfying	sl
Saturday	Sl
sauce	ss
save	sv
saver	svr
saving	svg
saw	s
say	sa
saying	sag
says	sz
scale	ska
scalp	skp
scandal	sk—l
scarce	sks
scare	ska
scene	se
scenic	sek

schedule	skjl
scheme	ske
scholar	sklr
scholarship	sklrzp
school	sku
science	s,
scientific	s—fk
scientist	s—S
scissors	szr
scope	sko
score	sko
scoring	skog
scorn	skn
scout	skwt
scramble	skmB
scrap	skp
scrape	ska
scratch	skc
scream	ske
screen	ske
screening	skeg
scrub	skb
scuff	skf
sculpture	skpcr
sea	c
seafood	cfu
seal	se
seamless	sels
search	sc
seashore	czo
season	czn
seasonal	cznl
seasoning	czng
seat	se
second	sk—
secondary	sk—y
secret	ckt
secretarial	sktrl
secretary	skty
secretly	cktl
section	skj
sectional	skjl
secure	sku
securing	skug
security	skut
see	c
seed	se
seeding	seg
seeing	c
seek	se
seeking	seg
seem	se
seen	c
segregate	sgga
segregation	sggj
seize	cz
seldom	sdm
select	slk

selecting	slkg
selection	slkj
selective	slkv
self	sf
sell	sl
seller	slr
selling	slg
semester	smsr
semiannual	smanl
seminar	smnr
senate	snl
senator	snlr
send	s—
sending	s—g
senior	cnr
sensational	snsjl
sense	s,
sensible	snsB
sent	s—
sentence	s—,
sentiment	s——
sentimental	s——l
separate (*adj.*)	sprl
separate (*vb.*)	spra
separately	sprll
separation	spry
September	Sp
sequel	cql
sequence	cq,
serial	srl
series	srz
serious	srx
sermon	smn
servant	sv—
serve	sv
service	svs
serviceman	svsmn
servicing	svsg
serving	svg
session	sj
set	sl
setting	slg
settle	sll
settlement	sll—
setup	slp
several	svrl
severe	sve
sew	so
sewage	sj
sewing	sog
sex	sx
shade	za
shadow	zdo
shaft	zf
shake	za
shall	zl
shame	za
shampoo	zmpu

shape	za	shop	zp
share	za	shopping	zpg
shareholder	zahdr	shore	zo
sharing	zag	short	z/
sharp	zp	shortage	z/j
shave	zv	shortcut	z/kt
she	z	shorten	z/n
shear	ze	shortest	z/s
shed	zd	shorthand	z/h
sheen	ze	shortly	z/l
sheer	ze	shot	zt
sheet	ze	should	zd
shelf	zf	shoulder	zdr
shell	zl	shout	zwt
shellac	zlk	shove	zv
shelter	zltr	shovel	zvl
sheriff	zrf	show	zo
shield	zd	showing	zog
shift	zf	shown	zon
shine	zi	showroom	zoru
ship	zp	shrink	zq
shipment	zp—	shrinkage	zqj
shipper	zpr	shrub	zb
shipping	zpg	shut	zt
shirt	z/	shutter	ztr
shock	zk	shy	zi
shoe	zu	sick	sk
shoot	zu	sickness	skns
shooting	zug	side	si

sidewalk	siwk	sink	sq
siding	sig	sinking	sqg
sift	sf	sir	sr
sight	si	siren	srn
sign	si	sister	sSr
signal	sgnl	sit	sl
signature	sgncr	site	si
signer	sir	situation	sil
significant	sgnfk—	situational	sil
signify	sgnfi	size	sz
silence	sl,	skate	ska
silent	sl—	sketch	skc
silently	sl—l	ski	ske
silk	sk	skid	skd
silver	svr	skill	skl
silverware	svrwa	skillful	sklf
similar	smlr	skin	skn
simmer	smr	skirt	sk/
simple	smpl	sky	ski
simplicity	smpsl	skyscraper	skiskar
simplify	smpfi	slack	sk
simply	smpl	slain	sa
simultaneously	smlnxl	slam	sm
since	s,	sleep	se
sincere	snse	slender	s—r
sincerely	snsel	slept	sp
sing	sg	slice	si
single	sgl	slide	si
singular	sglr	slight	si

slightly	sil	sofa	sfa
slim	sm	soft	sf
sling	sg	softener	sfnr
slip	sp	softness	sfns
slippery	spy	soil	syl
slogan	sgn	sold	sd
slope	so	soldier	sjr
slow	so	sole	so
slum	sm	solemn	slm
small	sml	solicit	slsl
smaller	smlr	solid	sld
smallest	smlS	solution	slj
smart	sm/	solve	sv
smash	smz	solvent	sv—
smear	sme	some	sm
smell	sml	somebody	smbd
smile	smi	someday	smD
smoke	smo	somehow	smhw
smooth	sm—	someone	smwn
snap	snp	something	sm—g
snug	sng	sometime	smti
so	o	somewhat	smwt
soak	so	somewhere	smwa
soap	so	son	sn
soar	so	song	sg
sober	sbr	soon	su
social	sx	sooner	sur
society	ssl	soothe	s—
soda	sda	sophomore	sfmo

sore	so
sorrow	sro
sorry	sy
sort	s/
sought	sl
sought-after	slaf
sound	s—
soup	su
sour	swr
source	ss
south	S
southeast	SE
southeastern	SEn
southern	Sn
southwest	SW
southwestern	SWn
souvenir	svne
space	spa
spacious	spx
span	spn
spare	spa
spark	sp/
sparkle	sp/l
speak	spe
speaker	sper
speaking	speg
special	spx
specialist	spxS
specialize	spxz
specially	spxl
specialty	spxl
specific	spc
specifically	spc
specification	spc
specify	spc
spectacular	spklklr
spectator	spkllr
speech	spc
speed	spe
speedometer	spdmlr
spelling	splg
spend	sp—
spending	sp—g
spent	sp—
spice	spi
spill	spl
spin	spn
spirit	sprl
spiritual	sprcl
spite	spi
splendid	sp—d
split	spl
spoil	spyl
spoke	spo
sponge	spnj
sponsor	spnsr
sponsoring	spnsrg
spool	spu

163

spoon	spu
sport	sp/
sporting	sp/g
sportsman	sp/mn
sportswear	sp/wa
spot	spt
spotless	sptls
spotlight	sptli
spouse	spws
spray	spa
spread	spd
spring	spg
springtime	spgti
sprinkle	spgl
spun	spn
spy	spi
square	sqa
squeeze	sqz
stability	Sbll
stabilization	SBzj
stable	SB
stack	Sk
stadium	Sdm
staff	Sf
stage	Sj
stain	Sa
stainless	Sals
stair	Sa
stairway	Sawa
stake	Sa
stalk	Sk
stall	Sl
stamp	Sm
stand	S—
standard	S—/
standardize	S—/z
standing	S—g
staple	Spl
stapling	Splg
star	Sr
starch	Sc
stare	Sa
start	S/
starting	S/g
starve	Sv
state	Sa
statement	Sa—
statesman	Samn
statewide	Sawi
stating	Sag
station	Sj
stationary	Sjy
stationery	Sjy
statistical	SlSkl
statistics	SlSx
status	Sls
statutory	Scly
staunch	Snc

stay	Sa
steadily	Sdl
steady	Sd
steal	Se
steam	Se
steamer	Ser
steamship	Sezp
steel	Se
steep	Se
steer	Se
stem	Sm
stencil	Snsl
steno	Sno
stenographer	Sngfr
stenographic	Sngfk
stenography	Sngfe
step	Sp
stereo	Sro
stereophonic	Srfnk
stern	Sn
stevedore	Svdo
stewardship	S/zp
stick	Sk
sticker	Skr
stiff	Sf
still	Sl
stimulate	Smla
stimulating	Smlag
sting	Sg

stipulate	Spla
stir	Sr
stitch	Sc
stitching	Scg
stock	Sk
stockholder	Skhdr
stocking	Skg
stole	So
stolen	Son
stomach	Smk
stone	So
stood	Sd
stool	Su
stop	Sp
stopping	Spg
storage	Sj
store	So
storekeeper	Soker
storm	Sm
stormy	Sme
story	Sy
stout	Swl
straight	Sa
straighten	San
strain	Sa
strange	Snj
stranger	Snjr
strap	Sp
strategy	Slg

stray	Sa
streak	Se
stream	Se
street	Se
strength	Sg—
strengthen	Sg-n
strenuous	Sns
stress	Ss
stretch	Sc
stricken	Skn
strict	Sk
strictly	Skl
stride	Si
strike	Si
string	Sg
strip	Sp
stripe	Si
strive	Sv
stroke	So
strong	Sg
stronger	Sgr
strongly	Sgl
struck	Sk
structure	Skcr
struggle	Sgl
stub	Sb
stucco	Sko
student	Sd—
studio	Sdo
study	Sd
studying	Sdg
stuff	Sf
stump	Sm
stupid	Spd
sturdy	Se
style	Si
subcontractor	sktkr
subdue	sd
subject	sjk
sublease	sle
sublet	slt
sublime	sli
submarine	smre
submerge	smj
submission	smj
submit	smt
subscribe	sski
subscriber	sskir
subscribing	sskig
subscription	sskpj
subsequent	ssq—
subside	ssi
subsidiary	ssdy
subsistence	ssS
substance	sS
substantial	sSnx
substantially	sSnxl
substitute	sStu

substitution	sSly	summarizing	smrzg
subtitle	sUl	summary	smy
subtract	slk	summer	smr
subtropical	slpkl	summit	sml
suburb	sb	summons	smn
suburban	sbn	sun	sn
subway	swa	sundae	s—a
succeed	skse	Sunday	Sn
succeeding	skseg	sundries	s—y
success	skss	sunny	sne
successful	skssf	sunrise	snrz
successfully	skssf	sunset	snsl
successive	skssv	sunshine	snzi
such	sc	super	spr
sudden	sdn	superb	spb
suddenly	sdnl	superficial	spfx
suede	swa	superintendent	spint—
suffer	sfr	superior	sprr
sufficient	sfz—	supervise	spvz
sufficiently	sfz—l	supervising	spvzg
sugar	zgr	supervision	spvj
suggest	sgjS	supervisor	spvzr
suggesting	sgjSg	supervisory	spvzy
suggestion	sgjsj	supper	spr
suicide	ssi	supplement	sp—
suit	su	supplemental	sp—l
suitable	suB	supplementary	sp—y
suite	swe	supplier	spir
sum	sm	supply	spi

supplying	sprg	suspense	ssp,
support	sp	suspension	sspnj
supporting	spg	suspicious	sspx
suppose	spz	sustain	sSa
supreme	spe	swallow	swlo
sure	zu	swamp	swm
surely	zul	sweater	swlr
surface	sfs	sweep	swe
surgeon	sjn	sweet	swe
surgery	sjy	swell	swl
surgical	sjkl	swerve	swv
surplus	sps	swim	swm
surprise	spz	swimming	swmg
surprising	spzg	swing	swg
surrender	sr—r	switch	swc
surround	sr—	switchboard	swcb
surrounding	sr—g	swung	swg
survey	sva	syllable	slB
surveyor	svar	symbol	smB
survival	svvl	sympathetic	smp—lk
survive	svv	sympathy	smp—e
survivor	svvr	symphony	smfne
suspect	sspk	synthetic	sn—lk
suspend	ssp—	system	sSm

T

tab	lb	tablespoon	lBspu
table	lB	tablet	lbl

tabulate	tbla	tavern	tvn
tabulating	tblag	tax	tx
tack	tk	taxable	txB
tackle	tkl	taxation	txj
tact	tk	taxi	txe
tactful	tkf	taxicab	txekb
tactic	tktk	taxpayer	txpar
tag	tg	tea	t
tail	ta	teach	tc
tailor	tlr	teacher	tcr
take	ta	teaching	tcg
taken	tan	team	te
taking	tag	tear (*n.*)	te
talent	tl—	tear (*vb.*)	ta
talk	tk	tease	tz
talkative	tkv	teaspoon	tspu
talking	tkg	technical	tknkl
tall	tl	technician	tknj
tame	ta	technique	tkne
tan	tn	tedious	tdx
tank	tq	teen-age	teaj
tap	tp	teen-ager	teajr
tape	ta	teeth	t—
tar	tr	telegram	tlgm
target	tgt	telegraph	tlgf
tariff	trf	telephone	tlfo
task	ts	television	tlvj
taste	tS	tell	tl
taught	tt	telling	tlg

temper	lmpr	than	—n
temperature	lmprcr	thank	—g
temporarily	lmprrl	thankful	—gf
temporary	lmpry	thankfully	—gf
tempt	lmp	thanking	—gg
tenant	ln—	that	—l
tend	l—	the	—
tendency	l—nc	theater	—lr
tennis	lns	theft	—f
tense	l,	their	—r
tension	lnj	them	—m
tent	l—	theme	—e
tentative	l—v	themselves	—msvz
tenure	lnr	then	—n
term	lm	theory	—y
terminal	lmnl	therapy	—rp
terminate	lmna	there	—r
termination	lmnj	thereafter	—raf
termite	lmi	thereby	—rb
terrible	lrB	therefore	—rf
territory	lrly	therein	—rn
terror	lrr	thereof	—rv
test	lS	thereon	—ro
testify	lSfi	thereto	—rl
testimony	lSmne	thermometer	—mmlr
text	lx	these	—z
textbook	lxbk	they	—a
textile	lxli	thick	—k
texture	lxcr	thickness	—kns

thief	—e	tide	li
thin	—n	tie	li
thing	—g	tier	le
think	—q	tight	li
thinking	—gg	tile	li
this	—s	till	ll
thorough	—ro	timber	lmbr
thoroughfare	—rofa	time	li
thoroughly	—rol	timely	lil
those	—oz	timetable	lilB
though	—o	timing	lig
thought	—l	tin	ln
thousand	—wz—	tint	l—
thread	—d	tiny	lne
threat	—l	tip	lp
threaten	—ln	tire	li
threw	—u	tissue	lzu
thrift	—f	title	ltl
thrill	—l	to	l
throat	—o	toast	lS
through	—u	toaster	lSr
throughout	—uo	tobacco	lbko
throughway	—uwa	today	lD
throw	—o	toe	lo
thrown	—on	together	lg—r
thunder	—r	toil	lyl
Thursday	Th	told	ld
thus	—s	toll	lo
ticket	tkl	tomorrow	lmro

ton
tone
tonight
too
took
tool
tooth
top
topic
tore
torn
tornado
toss
total
totally
touch
tough
tour
tourist
tow
toward
towel
tower
town
toy
trace
track
traction
tractor

trade
trademark
trading
tradition
traditional
traffic
tragedy
tragic
trail
trailer
train
training
transact
transaction
transcribe
transcript
transcription
transfer
transferable
transform
transformation
transfusion
transistor
transit
translate
translation
transmission
transmit
transparent

transplant	Tp—
transport	Tp/
transportation	Tp/t
transporting	Tp/g
trap	lp
trash	lz
travel	lvl
traveling	lvlg
tray	la
tread	ld
treasure	lzr
treasurer	lzrr
treasury	lzy
treat	le
treating	leg
treatment	le—
treaty	ll
tree	le
tremendous	l—s
tremendously	l—sl
trend	l—
trespassing	lspsg
trial	li
tribute	lbu
trick	lk
trim	lm
trip	lp
triple	lpl
triplicate	lpkl
triumph	lmf
troops	lu
trophy	lfe
tropical	lpkl
trouble	lB
truce	lu
truck	lk
trucking	lkg
true	lu
truly	lul
trunk	lq
trust	lS
trustee	lSe
trustfully	lSf
trusting	lSg
truth	l—
try	li
trying	lig
tub	lb
tube	lu
tubeless	luls
tuberculosis	lbklss
Tuesday	Ts
tug	lg
tuition	lj
tune	lu
tunnel	lnl
turf	lf
turkey	lve

173

turmoil	lmyl
turn	ln
turnout	lno
turnover	lnv
turnpike	lnpi
tutor	llr
twice	lwi
twin	lwn
twine	lwi
twist	lw$
type	li
typewriter	lrir
typewriting	lrig
typical	lpkl
typing	lig
typist	li$

U

umbrella	umbla
unable	uaß
unanimously	unnmsl
unattended	ual_
unauthorized	ua_rz
unbend	ub_
unbreakable	ubaß
uncertain	us^r
unchanged	ucnj
unclaimed	uka
uncle	ugl
uncomfortable	ukfß
uncommon	ukmn
unconcerned	uksn
unconditional	ukdyl
unconscious	ukx
uncut	ukl
under	U
undergo	Ug
undergraduate	Uggl
underground	Ug_
undermine	Um
underprivileged	Upvlj
understand	U$_
understanding	U$_g
understood	U$d
undertake	Ula
undertaken	Ulan
undertaking	Ulag
undertone	Ulo
underworld	Uwd
underwrite	Uri
underwriting	Urig
undesirable	udziß
undetermined	udlmn
undiscovered	udkvr

undivided	udvz
undo	ud
undoubtedly	udwll
uneasy	uez
unemployed	umpy
unequal	uegl
uneven	uev
unexpected	uxpk
unexplored	uxpo
unfair	ufa
unfavorable	ufvrB
unfed	ufd
unfilled	ufl
unforeseen	ufc
unfortunate	ufcnl
unfortunately	ufcnll
ungracious	ugx
unhappy	uhp
unharmed	uhm
unheard	uh/
unhurt	uh/
uniform	unfm
uniformity	unfml
uninterested	uNs
union	unn
unique	une
unit	unl
unite	uni
united	uni

universal	unvsl
university	unvsl
unknown	unn
unlawful	ulaf
unleash	ulz
unless	uls
unlighted	uli
unlike	uli
unlikely	ulil
unlimited	ulml
unlined	uli
unload	ulo
unloading	ulog
unmarried	umy
unnatural	uncrl
unnecessary	unssy
unobserved	uobsv
unofficial	uofx
unorganized	uog
unpaid	upa
unpleasant	upz
unprecedented	upsd
unpredictable	updkB
unrealistic	urlsk
unreasonable	urznB
unreliable	urliB
unrest	urs
unrestricted	ursk
unsafe	usa

unseen	uc	upset	psl
unshipped	uzp_	upward	p/
unspoken	uspon	urge	uj
unstable	uSB	urgent	uj—
unsuccessful	uskssf	urgently	uj—l
unsurpassed	usps_	urging	ujg
untidy	uld	us	s
until	ull	usage	usj
untimely	ulil	use (*n.*)	us
unto	ul	use (*vb.*)	uz
unused	uuz_	useful	usf
unusual	uuzl	useless	usls
unwholesome	uhosm	user	uzr
up	p	using	uzg
upheld	phd	usual	uzl
upholstered	phSr_	usually	uzll
upholstering	phSrg	utensils	ulnsl
upholstery	phSy	utility	ulll
upon	pn	utilize	ullz
upper	pr	utmost	ulmS

V

vacancy	vknc	vain	va
vacation	vkj	valid	vld
vaccinate	vksna	valley	vl
vaccine	vkse	valuable	vluB
vacuum	vku	value	vlu
vague	va	valve	vv

van	vn
vandalism	v-lzm
vanish	vnz
vanquish	vgqz
variable	vyB
variance	vy,
variety	vrl
various	vrx
varnish	vnz
varsity	vsl
vary	vy
vast	vS
vault	vl
vegetable	vjlB
vehicle	vkl
veil	va
vein	va
vending	v-g
vendor	v-r
veneer	vne
venetian	vnj
ventilate	v-la
ventilator	v-lar
venture	vncr
verdict	v^k
verification	vrfkj
verify	vrfi
version	vj
vertical	v^kl
very	v
vessel	vsl
vest	vS
veteran	vlrn
veterinarian	vlrnrn
via	va
viaduct	vdk
vibration	vbj
vice	vs
vice-president	vspzd-
vicinity	vsnl
vicious	vx
victim	vklm
victorious	vklrx
victory	vkly
video	vdo
view	vu
viewer	vur
vigilance	vjl,
vigor	vgr
vigorous	vgrs
vigorously	vgrsl
village	vlj
violation	vlj
violence	vl,
virtually	vcll
virtue	vcu
visibility	vzbll
visible	vzB

vision	vj
visit	vzl
visiting	vzlg
visual	vzl
vital	vll
vitally	vlll
vitamin	vlmn
vivid	vvd
vocal	vkl
vocation	vkj
vocational	vkjl
voice	vys
void	vyd
volume	vlu
voluntary	vl—y
volunteer	vl—e
vote	vo
voter	vor
voting	vog
voucher	vwcr
vow	vw
vowel	vwl

W

wage	wj
wagon	wgn
wait	wa
waiting	wag
waitress	was
waive	wv
wake	wa
walk	wk
wall	wl
wallet	wll
wallpaper	wlppr
walnut	wnl
wander	w—r
want	w—
war	wo
ward	/
wardrobe	/ro
ware	wa
warehouse	wahws
warehouseman	wahwsmn
warm	wm
warmer	wmr
warn	wn
warning	wng
warrant	wr—
warranty	wrnl
wartime	woli
was	z
wash	wz
washable	wzB

washer	wzr
washing	wzg
waste	ws
watch	wc
watchful	wcf
watchfully	wcf
watchmaker	wcmar
watchman	wcmn
water	wlr
waterfront	wlrf—
waterproof	wlrpu
wave	wv
way	wa
wayward	wa/
wax	wx
we	w
weak	we
weakness	wens
wealth	w—
weapon	wpn
wear	wa
weather	w—r
weave	wv
wedding	wdg
wedge	wj
Wednesday	Wd
weed	we
week	W
weekday	WD
weekend	W—
weekly	Wl
weigh	wa
weighing	wag
weight	wa
welcome	lk
weld	wd
welfare	lfa
well	l
went	w—
were	w
west	W
western	Wn
wet	wl
wharf	wf
what	wl
whatever	wlev
wheat	we
wheel	we
when	wn
whenever	wnev
where	wa
whereas	waz
whereby	wab
wherever	waev
whether	w—r
which	wc
whichever	wcev
while	wi

whip	wp
whisper	wspr
whistle	wsl
white	wi
who	w
whoever	wev
whole	ho
wholesale	hosa
wholesaler	hosar
whom	w
whose	wz
why	y
wide	wi
widely	wil
wider	wir
widespread	wispd
widow	wdo
width	wd—
wife	wi
wig	wg
wild	yd
will	l
willing	lg
willpower	lpwr
win	wn
wind (*n.*)	w—
wind (*vb.*)	y—
window	w—o
windshield	w—zd

wine	wi
wing	wg
winner	wnr
winning	wng
winter	w—r
wipe	wi
wiper	wir
wire	wi
wiring	wig
wisdom	wzdm
wise	yz
wish	wz
wistfully	wsf
with	w—
withdraw	w—da
withdrawal	w—dal
withdrawn	w—dan
withheld	w—hd
withholding	w—hdg
within	w—n
without	w—f
withstand	wS—
witness	wlns
witty	wl
woman	wmn
women	wmn
won	wn
wonder	w—r
wonderful	w—rf

wonderfully	w—f	worth	w—
wondering	w—rg	worthwhile	w—wi
wood	wd	worthy	w—e
wooden	wdn	would	wd
wool	wl	wound	w—
woolen	wln	woven	wvn
word	w/	wrap	rp
wording	w/g	wrapper	rpr
wore	wo	wrapping	rpg
work	w/	wreck	rk
workable	w/B	wreckage	rkj
worker	w/r	wringer	rgr
working	w/g	wrinkle	rgl
workman	w/mn	wrist	rS
workshop	w/zp	write	ri
world	wd	writer	rir
worn	won	writing	rig
worry	wy	written	rtn
worse	ws	wrong	rg
worst	wS	wrote	ro

X

X-ray	xra	xylophone	zlfo

Y

yacht	yl	year	Y
yard	y/	yearly	Yl

yell	yl
yellow	ylo
yes	ys
yesterday	ySrD
yet	yl
yield	yd
you	u
young	yg
younger	ygr
youngster	ygSr
your	u
yours	u
yourself	usf
youth	u—

Z

zero	zro
zip	zp
zipper	zpr
zone	zo